16.95

D0078542

Teachers' Pets, Troublemakers, and Nobodies

Recent Titles in
Contributions in Afro-American and African Studies
Series Adviser: Hollis R. Lynch

Red Over Black: Black Slavery Among the Cherokee Indians
R. Halliburton, Jr.

New Rulers in the Ghetto: The Community Development Corporation and Urban Poverty
Harry Edward Berndt

Black Ethos: Northern Urban Life and Thought, 1890-1930
David Gordon Nielson

The FLN in Algeria: Party Development in a Revolutionary Society
Henry F. Jackson

Old Roots in New Lands: Historical and Anthropological Perspectives on Black Experiences in the Americas
Ann M. Pescatello, editor

Africans and Seminoles: From Removal to Emancipation
Daniel F. Littlefield, Jr.

American Socialism and Black Americans: From the Age of Jackson to World War II
Philip S. Foner

Black Academic Libraries and Research Collections: An Historical Survey
Jessie Carney Smith

The American Slave: A Composite Autobiography, Supplementary Series
George P. Rawick, editor

Trabelin' On: The Slave Journey to an Afro-Baptist Faith
Mechal Sobel

Revisiting Blassingame's *The Slave Community:* The Scholars Respond
Al-Tony Gilmore, editor

The "Hindered Hand": Cultural Implications of Early African-American Fiction
Arlene A. Elder

The Cherokee Freedmen: From Emancipation to American Citizenship
Daniel F. Littlefield, Jr.

Teachers' Pets, Troublemakers, and Nobodies

BLACK CHILDREN IN ELEMENTARY SCHOOL

Helen Gouldner,
with the assistance of
Mary Symons Strong

Contributions in Afro-American and African Studies, Number 41

GREENWOOD PRESS
Westport, Connecticut • London, England

Library of Congress Cataloging in Publication Data

Gouldner, Helen P
    Teachers' pets, troublemakers, and nobodies.

    (Contributions in Afro-American and African studies ;
no. 41 0069-9624)
      Includes index.
      Bibliography: p.
      1. Afro-Americans--Education (Elementary)
2. Students' socio-economic status--United States.
I. Strong, Mary Symons. II. Title.
LC2771.G68   372.9'73   78-53660
ISBN 0-313-20417-9

Material from Ray C. Rist, *The Urban School: A Factory
for Failure* (Cambridge: The MIT Press, 1973) is re-
printed with the permission of the MIT Press.

Library of Congress Catalog Card Number: 78-53660
ISBN: 0-313-20417-9
ISSN: 0069-9624

First published in 1978

Greenwood Press, Inc.
51 Riverside Avenue, Westport, Connecticut 06880

Printed in the United States of America

10 9 8 7 6 5 4 3 2 1

**TO
ANDY**

CONTENTS

TABLES

PREFACE

The research on which this book is largely based was designed by
Jules Henry and conducted by him during the first nine months of
the research project, until he became incapacitated by illness. His
subsequent death meant that he could not finish the work he had
begun, but when the enterprise was carried on by others, every attempt was made to reflect his concerns with the influence of American culture on the children of our schools. It would be difficult to
fully express the debt owed Jules Henry for the original ideas and
the methodology incorporated by him into what turned out to be
the last of his many contributions to the literature on culture and
personality.

David J. Pittman took on the responsibilities of directing the
research in 1968, with John Bennett and Irving Louis Horowitz serving as assistant directors. In 1969, Helen Gouldner became director and, with John Bennett continuing as assistant director, served
until the project's termination in 1971. John Bennett played a major role both in guiding the research and in assuring its continuity.
Marshall Durbin, who became a consultant to the project in 1970,
worked closely with several of the research assistants and provided
guidance in some preliminary studies in linguistics.

Glen Akers, Jeffrey Gilbert, Steven Jones, Elizabeth Ann
McPike, Marco M. Pardi, Ray C. Rist, Patricia Anne Roberts,
Mark Schoepfle, Thomas Shapiro, Carol S. Talbert, and Bruce
Zelkovitz were research assistants for varying lengths of time. The
difficulties of their tasks were compounded by the necessarily frequent changes in personnel among not only the directors but also
among the research assistants themselves, some of whom were

drafted for military service. Particular contributions were made by Carol Talbert and Ray Rist. While continuing her own research, Carol Talbert helped maintain continuity during the various periods of transition by training and orienting new research assistants, organizing seminars, and writing a number of papers which she delivered at professional meetings. Ray Rist completed his Ph.D. dissertation while on the project and contributed in many ways to various phases of the work.

Several other individuals are due special thanks for their assistance. Alaine Arndt was generous in sharing her ideas, criticisms, and alternative interpretations of the data with the author. L. Leon Campbell, Provost and Vice President for Academic Affairs at the University of Delaware, provided a fellow administrator with encouragement and support to complete the manuscript. In a sense, the authorship of the book is shared by Mary Symons Strong, whose knowledge of the field and editorial skills made a technical report come alive.

Finally, acknowledgment is due the United States Office of Education for their funding of the research project (Contract no. OEC-3-7-062771-2714).

Helen Gouldner
Newark, Delaware
May 1978

Teachers' Pets, Troublemakers, and Nobodies

CHAPTER

1 The Natural History of a School Career

"Darnell Martin brought a turtle to school this morning. He is a discoverer." Thirty-one pairs of eyes focus on these words as Mrs. Bobb prints them on the blackboard in large, even letters. The pupils glance occasionally from the blackboard to the cardboard box containing the turtle Darnell had carried to school for Show and Tell. "Now, children, copy the sentences on your papers and don't forget about your heading." The children won't forget. They already know the routine. They must write four things at the top of their sheets of lined paper before copying what Mrs. Bobb put on the board. The name of the school is to appear on the first line, the date on the second, their "reading level" on line three, and their own name on line four.

The first graders lean over their papers and begin working on the four-line heading. Some zip through the entire assignment and finish before Mrs. Bobb adds another instruction: "Draw a picture of the turtle in the center of the page." But at this point most of the children are still struggling to finish their headings. Some have copied the first three lines from another spot on the blackboard, but are having trouble printing their own last names. Others create a hopeless scrawl of jumbled letters on all four lines.

Every day, the same children run afoul of the insurmountable barrier of the heading, but Mrs. Bobb never varies the assignment or its format. A few of the children get up and approach the teacher at her desk to ask for help. Her response is to tell them to go to their seats and practice their letters. Meanwhile, she stays in her seat at the front of the room, correcting papers and keeping order from a distance, repeating her commands to the children to sit down and finish up their papers.

All of the children are working at their seats now—all except three of the girls, Patricia, Shirley, and Sheila, and two of the boys, Gerry and James. These five pupils are the first to finish their papers and are out of their seats and walking up and down the rows, acting as teacher's helpers. Some of the pupils ask them for help, but when other children who have finished, but have not been designated as helpers, respond to their seatmates' requests for assistance, Mrs. Bobb tells them to stop bothering their neighbors and splits them up when they persist. Only the five helpers are permitted to help.

Mrs. Bobb turns from her work and speaks to an adult who is present in the classroom as an observer from a research study. Complaining in a fatigued voice about the endless time it takes to correct her pupils' papers, Mrs. Bobb explains, "Sometimes it gets so bad, the kids just have to finish their work without my telling them whether they did any good at all."

At this point Patricia walks down the aisle to the back of her row to help Reginald. She takes his left hand in which he holds his pencil and tries to guide it to form the letters on the page. Reginald tightens his hold on the pencil, keeping his arm rigid. He resists the pressure of her hand while looking off in another direction with a vacant expression on his face. But Patricia persists in trying to get him to move the pencil. She finally gives up in disgust, glowering at him as she leaves his desk. As she passes by the desk of another boy, David, he gets up and holds his pencil out to her. She sneers and bats it away, and David sits back down in his seat showing no reaction on his face to what Patricia has done.

At this point only a few of the children are still working on their papers. Patricia goes down the aisle to the desk of another boy. Suddenly she jerks the paper away from him, scowling. The boy looks up at her in apparent surprise. She walks around to the front of the room and over to Mrs. Bobb, showing her the paper, pointing out how bad it is, saying it is impossible to make him do it right. Mrs. Bobb responds, "You'll have to help him with it. That's what you're here for."

Patricia returns again to Reginald's desk. She stands over him and tries once more to guide his hand but he continues to resist the pressure of her hand and arm. Patricia picks up the paper angrily and tears it into several pieces. Looking up, Mrs. Bobb says, "Honey, what are you doing to that boy's paper?" Then she speaks to Reginald, calling out his name. "Yes, Mrs. Bobb," he responds in a downtrodden voice. "What has happened to your paper?" Mrs. Bobb asks. Reginald replies in an accusing tone, "She tore it up." "Well, you get a new piece," she answers. He gets up, walks to the storage cabinet and takes out another sheet of paper. Patricia yells "fatso" at him. Two of his male classmates pester him, and he turns to Mrs. Bobb for help. She refuses, saying, "Well, if you were doing your work, you wouldn't be meddling with them, would you? You get back and do your work."

Now Gerry gets up and walks down the aisle. He stops and chats with Patricia. They are both laughing. Patricia goes back to Reginald. She takes his left hand again and begins to guide it against his will. The pencil slips off the paper, making a long erratic line across the sheet. Reginald exclaims frantically, "You did it! You made me go off the side of the paper." Patricia snaps at him, "No, I didn't. You lying." She walks to another desk and gets an eraser and tries to rub out the line. Unable to erase it, she takes Reginald's paper, turns it over, places it back on his desk, and walks off. Reginald turns around, calling after her in a distracted tone, "But, Patricia...."

Meanwhile, Shirley tries to help Tony. She becomes exasperated and writes the words for him instead of helping him do it himself. Mrs. Bobb notices this and tells her, "Shirley, hold his hand." At the same time, Patricia is holding another boy's hand. This boy resists, too. When he makes the *i* in his name too long, she rebukes him, "There, you did it again. I'm going to have to get an eraser." She walks over to another desk and takes an eraser from a boy who protests in vain. Patricia looks again at the first boy's paper and states flatly, "You ain't doing it right." The boy looks up, says nothing, and turns back to writing. She grabs the pencil from his hand and taunts him, "Now you can't write until I give it back." The boy looks up at her, shrugs his shoulders, reaches into his desk and pulls out the broken tip of an old pencil. Barely able to keep the lead from slipping out of his grasp, he continues writing.

By now most of the children have stopped working on their papers. The boy seated in the last desk of the fifth row stares at the jumble of letters which he has written as his heading. On the first line is *WODNO*. Under that, on the second line, are three unintelligible letters. Below them is *SRO*.

Reginald is starting on his second piece of paper. He writes *REGI* and stops. Gerry walks back to Reginald's desk, takes Reginald's pencil in his own hand, and writes *REGINALD*, saying "Come on, you do that." Reginald shakes his head hopelessly and says, "I can't yet." Gerry shows him again, "You hold it like this," and warns him impatiently, "Say there, boy, I'm gonna pants you." Trying to mold Reginald's fingers around the pencil, Gerry says harshly, "I told you. I ain't playin'." Reginald still resists. Gerry hits him on the shoulder and walks on, after which Reginald holds the pencil and makes a small *n*. Gerry moves over to Tony and picks up his pencil. Like Shirley, Gerry declines to hold Tony's hand to help him write the letters. Instead, Gerry writes the letters for him. Tony is not paying any attention. He drums his fingers and looks off in another direction.

Meanwhile, Sheila has also been walking up and down the aisles. As she goes past Erin, he shows her his paper. She glances at it and, with a look of disdain, walks on by. Erin shrugs his shoulders, a gesture which Sheila catches in the corner of her eye. She turns back scowling, points to the word *DISCOVERER* which Erin has crowded against the right edge of the paper. She jabs her finger toward it and says, "That's no good." Erin turns away acting as though he had expected Sheila to do that all along, his expression totally blank.[1]

This lesson period occurred in a classroom in an all-black elementary school in a large Midwestern city. It is plain to see that the children who were chosen by the teacher to be her helpers were having an experience in first grade which was very different from that of the children who failed to gain admission into the charmed circle of teacher preference. The social, psychological, and educational content of the time spent in school was strikingly dissimilar for the two groups. It appeared to be filled with rewards and satisfactions for a few pupils, but not for the remainder who were regularly submitted to belittlement and boredom.

Patricia, Gerry, Sheila, Shirley, and sometimes James—an appointed few—are free to walk around the room, a privilege denied to the other pupils. This right is augmented by a grant of authority from the teacher to supervise many of the other children. Patricia was seen taking things from other children with impunity, ignoring any pleas to return their possessions. As an arm of the teacher, she also had the prerogative to condemn the work of other pupils. She and the other favorites are allowed to control their classmates to the point of holding their hands—acts homologous to the teacher's insistence upon learning to control one's muscles and do "exactly as told." In addition, Mrs. Bobb engages Patricia in an act of dehumanizing Reginald by discussing his failures in his presence. When Patricia humiliates Reginald by tearing up his paper, the teacher tells him to get another sheet, but fails to reprimand Patricia, thereby exonerating her for a misdeed and meting out unequal treatment for misbehavior to another child in the same class.

Reginald knows that he cannot count on Mrs. Bobb to protect him from the unfair behavior of her helpers. Consequently, he resorts to a survival strategy of the weak—denial and passive resistance. He refuses to allow Patricia to guide his hand. The rigidity of his arm expresses the depth of his resentment. By staring off into space, moreover, he refuses to even acknowledge her attempt to help him. Making explicit the difference in her regard for Patricia and Reginald, Mrs. Bobb addresses Patricia as "honey" and Reginald merely as "boy." Some of the other boys, less able than Reginald to defend themselves, engage in passive acceptance rather than resistance as their response to the conditions they face in the classroom.

Could this kind of experience in the early grades possibly not contribute to or detract from the performance of children in school? Initially, the answer seems rather obvious. Of course, it does. The teachers' pets will do well. The rest will limp along. But does this actually happen? And why is it that one child is selected as a teacher's pet over another? Is this blatant preference for some children and neglect of others characteristic of teachers other than Mrs. Bobb?

These questions are important to answer when we are confronted with the puzzling fact that many black children do not learn how to read as early or as well as they should. Many perfectly normal children never learn to read at all. Why is it that some black children succeed in ghetto schools, but many others fail? The prevalence of academic retardation and failure among black students has become a national educational problem, a seemingly intractable one. Large numbers of ghetto youth of school age are not even in school—they are either pushed out or drop out. Those who stay often learn so little that they leave as functional illiterates.

In an effort to explain the dismal results of public school education in the ghettos of the major American cities, two major perspectives emerged in the sixties. One view located the problem in the child himself and asked "how the child can be changed to fit the school's definition of achievement."[2] It focused on the characteristics of ghetto children—the backgrounds, preparation, attitudes, and cognitive abilities which they brought to school with them. The most general assumption was that their cognitive growth, the development of their perceptual abilities and their language skills had been stunted in the so-called culturally deprived environment of ghetto homes and neighborhoods. This perspective, which was labeled by Kenneth B. Clark in *Dark Ghetto* as the "cult of cultural deprivation," was criticized for incorrectly blaming inner-city children and their backgrounds for the widespread academic retardation in ghetto schools—for making the victims of poor education into its agents.[3]

While not denying the impact of extraschool factors, a second perspective shifted the focus of responsibility for the abominable reading and arithmetic scores of black children to the schools themselves. Emphasis was placed on the need to hold the schools accountable for their failure to educate ghetto children. It criticized the lack of adaptability and flexibility in the organizational structure of ghetto schools, and questioned the competence and commitment of the teachers. Arthur Pearl, for example, pointed out that it was "important to examine the attributes of schooling which could conceivably be driving youth out of education."[4] Others noted that it seemed reasonable to assume that the failure of many ghetto children was the result of their teachers' attitudes and behavior toward them.

The debate goes on. Some continue to blame the schools and the teacher. Others claim that the children are uneducable. But one

thing is certain: black children in ghetto schools are not a homo-
geneous group, either when they enter or leave school. This is frequently lost sight of when making comparisons between black and
white pupils. Both sets of students lose their individual identities
when they are lumped together in groups as though they were un-
differentiated masses.

Every child has an individual school history which is his and his
alone. The nature of the school experience of Patricia and
Reginald, for example, could not be more different. The lengthy
school history of the average American child starts on the first day
of kindergarten and unfolds day by day as he passes from grade to
grade and from teacher to teacher until he leaves the classroom at a
legally permissible or later age. As he goes through the school system, many things happen to him that affect his individual history
of performance as a student. If someone were at his side watching
this experience as it occurred from minute to minute, if someone
were almost as intimately acquainted with the child's life at school
and at home as the child was, the steps the child took that led him
on the road to success or failure in his schoolwork could be docu-
mented while it was taking place.

A research project was set up to try to deepen our acquaintance
with the ghetto child's early years in school and at home. The study
was sponsored by the United States Office of Education which in-
vited the anthropologist Jules Henry to design and carry out a
study which was eventually known as "The Natural History of the
Education of the Black Child in the City."[5] A team of researchers
was organized to observe as much as possible at firsthand about the
personal experience of being a black child in a ghetto school. The
plan involved having observers spend enough time with black children in their classrooms and at home to know them as individuals.
Its aim was to concentrate on the experiences of particular children,
to grasp the nature of their lives, and to account for their particular
success or failure in school while it was happening. The children
were pupils in four all-black schools. For purposes of comparison,
white children in two upper-middle-class schools in a suburb of the
same city and in one working-class school in a nearby smaller city
were included in the observations.

From the first day of school in September when the students

entered kindergarten until three years later when some of them had finished second grade, researchers from the study project were regularly present in selected classrooms of the four ghetto schools. These research team members also visited the homes of some of the children and talked with their parents, grandparents, brothers, sisters, and whoever else happened to be there. While in the children's homes, they paid special attention to how the children interacted with their parents, siblings, and friends. In the classrooms, they watched the emergence of either the behavior of success or the behavior of failure in the individual child. The drama of the children's young lives was played out before the observers' eyes. Unhappily, the ways of failure at schoolwork were learned by the children much more frequently than the ways of success.

Naturalistic Observation

Jules Henry, the anthropologist who initiated the research project and was its principal investigator at the outset, designed the research along the lines he had used earlier in his studies of families, schools, and homes for the aged and had reported in his book, *Culture Against Man.*[6] His methodology grew out of a highly personalized conception of research, one in which the investigator spends a great deal of time observing subjects in their "natural habitat" without participating in their activities. Called naturalistic observation or nonparticipant observation, the method was employed again in this project. Henry sent a team of researchers into the classrooms and homes of black children with instructions to observe and note as much as possible about everything they heard and saw without becoming a part of what was going on. Since Henry thought that the interaction between the child and the teacher in the classroom would be critical, he instructed the researchers to start out with that as their primary focus. Later, other pairs of interactors were added. As head of the research, Henry worked very closely with the observers in the field, constantly reviewing their written observations and discussing their reactions, feelings, perceptions, and intuitions.

Although not dissimilar from some techniques used by anthropologists, Henry's kind of naturalistic observation departs sharply from the more traditional methods of collecting data employed by social scientists when studying people in urban settings. For one thing, it does not involve the development of specific hypotheses—although instructions to the researchers as to what to look for suggest that there actually were implicit hypotheses. Nor does it include the collection of structured data from written questionnaires or other means of testing hypotheses. However, coding schemes for measuring interaction were developed and used by the observers. The main claim to scientific validity of naturalistic observation depends on the gathering of large quantities of qualitative data by a well-trained and sensitive field staff and the subsequent interpretation of the material by, in Jules Henry's case, a scholar of great insight and ability.

These interpretive abilities are critical to the success of this research method because it depends very heavily on one person being able to organize and make sense of observations of other field workers. When Jules Henry became seriously ill during the early stages of the field observations and subsequently died, the project lost his unique talents as interpreter and was, therefore, forced to change and add to the research methodology. The ultimate choice of methods of data collection and analyses represents a compromise between the direction of the research begun by Henry and the interests and skills of the staff who took over during his illness and after his death. The debt of the research group to Jules Henry was nowhere more keenly felt than in the certainty that there were more things to be seen in the data than his successors had discovered and that he most certainly would have found them, were he still alive.

As initially designed by Jules Henry, it was intended that the longitudinal study would be carried on for three years and develop in a series of steps in three phases. Phase 1, to begin in the first year, was to consist of five steps: (1) observation of Negro kindergartens, (2) selection of particular kindergarten children for observation, (3) concentration on observation of selected children in their classrooms, (4) observation of selected children in their homes, and (5) observation of selected children in their peer groups.

In Phase 2, to begin in the second year (first grade), the design called for observing the same children in the same situations. In Phase 3, to begin in the third year (second grade), the design called for continuing observations of these same children and adding a study of the "school culture." In a very general sense, the project followed this three-year model, although only one classroom was observed in the second grade.[7]

Observers in the Classroom

The bulk of the material collected by the project staff was obtained from observations in four different schools in one school district. These schools, which were entirely black, were assigned to the research project by the director of instruction in the city school system after considerable consultation. There is no evidence that the schools were in any way atypical of black schools in the school system; however, according to the director of instruction, they were "less studied than others." It was also noted that many of the teachers preferred a position in one of these schools to an assignment farther downtown in housing-project schools. In the schools chosen for study there was some variation in the socioeconomic backgrounds of the pupils in some of the classrooms under observation. A few of the children were from middle-class families, although a majority came from families who were either of the working poor or on welfare. So the difference between these schools and those schools serving the center of the inner city should be kept in mind.

During the first year of the project the researchers observed a kindergarten class in their assigned schools twice a week starting the opening day of school in the fall. Each class visit lasted one and one-half hours. Although the researchers took note of everything that happened in the classroom during these sessions, the primary focus of their observations was on the interaction between the teacher and the children. Stress was placed on making a continual, verbatim, handwritten record of everything said by both the teacher and the children—especially on the teacher's instructions, the boys' and girls' responses to these directions, and the teacher's reactions to their responses. The researchers took detailed notes on the students' answers to the teacher's questions during recitation—

both correct and incorrect—and how they were dealt with by the teacher. An attempt was made to record the name of the child, the exact content of the interaction, and the expression and tone of voice of both teacher and child. When observing the teacher, the researchers paid attention to her movements and facial gestures as well as to her words and tone of voice in an effort to describe the classroom atmosphere she created and to uncover any double messages from teacher to pupils, that is, where the teacher's behavior conveyed a meaning which differed from her actual words. It was assumed that the teacher's actions usually carried negative or positive valence for the child and that it was possible to code and count such actions. At least once every 15 minutes of the observation period, the observers noted the behavior of the class as a whole by taking an overall scan and recording such things as the noise level in the classroom and the mood and attentiveness of the students.

Although the main emphasis of the observations was on teacher-child interchanges, the researchers also noted conversations between the pupils. Having obtained permission from the teacher to move about the room freely, the researchers often sat very close to the children—occasionally, even on the floor with them. However, the researchers were careful not to interrupt the lessons—they were as unobstrusive as possible, observing but not taking part in any classroom activity. Verbal interchanges between the researchers and the children were avoided as much as possible in the classroom. According to all of the researchers, it was not long before the children seemed to treat them as though they were "pieces of furniture," although the teachers appeared to remain more conscious of their presence.

It cannot be assumed that any one of these classrooms was ever completely natural in the presence of the visitors, but because the children were unaware of the research aims connected with having outsiders in their classrooms, they could not tailor their behavior to fit any special expectations and, consequently, probably forced the teacher to behave in rather normally patterned ways. The children were probably on their good behavior or showing off for strangers in the beginning, but in time the frequent presence in the room of the same adult visitor seemed to be absorbed into the routine of the school day.

The researchers supplemented their observations of the teachers in their classrooms in two ways. In addition to conducting formal interviews with the teachers, using predesigned questions, the field staff also engaged them in many casual conversations about the progress of their students, school activities, methods and philosophies of teaching, and many other topics. As often as not the conversations were initiated by the teachers. The researchers also visited almost all of the teachers in their homes.

Early in the school year each kindergarten teacher was asked to select four children—two who would do well in school and two others who would do poorly (a boy and girl in each group). The choice and its criteria were left entirely to the teacher. The ghetto teachers had no difficulty making these selections. In one suburban middle-class school, however, the teachers said it was not possible to make such choices and insisted that all of the children would succeed. One of these suburban teachers told a researcher that she assumed that all of the children would eventually learn the curriculum and added that "We have many that will do very well." If the pupils had any problems with their schoolwork, she explained, there would be only temporary difficulties, possibly caused by an emotional problem at home, and such difficulties would be cleared up through counseling. This teacher refused to make the choice herself but finally agreed to the random selection of four children.

Another teacher in a suburban school was very worried about the aspect of the research that involved observations in the homes of the children who were to be selected. She explained:

You know these parents get upset at the least little thing or at the least little sign that something is wrong. Even if something is not wrong, they would still become suspicious. . . . For instance, Raymond . . . they've been to see a psychiatrist and they have all those other problems and I don't know but what they might wonder, "Well, why was I picked out?" And you know, Warren. There's been a divorce in the family. This is one of the things that upset me at first about picking the children. I didn't know how we were going to do this or what the parents would say. Our principal is going to talk to the superintendent over all the schools in this suburb and they will decide among themselves who should be recommended.[8]

The reluctance of the suburban teachers to take part in making choices which suggested that they could predict success and failure in their pupils was not expressed by the ghetto teachers. Possibly the ease with which they were able to select potential "high" and "low" achievers was related in part to the greater heterogeneity of the pupil population in the ghetto classrooms than in the middle-class suburban schools. Although lacking the data to make exact comparisons between the suburban and ghetto schools, all of the researchers found a noticeable range of difference in dress, income level, experience, and preparation for school of the children in the black kindergartens. Some of the children were, by any criteria one might choose, from middle-class families, while others in the same classroom were obviously from families living at the poverty line or below. Although the white suburban schoolchildren also came from families with a considerable range of income, going from medium to very high, it was harder to distinguish these children by their dress, speech, and other personal characteristics. They all looked middle class.

After the teachers had selected the four children in their classrooms who would do well and do poorly, or in the case of the suburban classrooms, after four children in each classroom had been selected randomly or by the principal, each researcher paid special attention to these children during classroom observations, although interaction between the teacher and all the students in the room remained the primary focus. In late November and early December of the first year, the project team started to visit the homes of the selected boys and girls. Over the three years of the research, members of the field staff made 180 home visits with 28 families. The number and length of the visits varied with the individual family, depending on the ease or difficulty of making arrangements for the appointments. In some cases it was hard to fit the visits into the work schedules of the parents, many of whom worked night shifts. Other families who lived in the city proved to be very difficult to locate at all.

At the time of the first visit in a child's home, a field staff member explained the purpose of the research to the child's mother, telling her that the university was making a study of their child's school, knew the child's teacher, was interested in how boys and girls learn in school, and wanted to talk with the parents about school and their children. In asking if they could visit them regularly, it was made clear to the parents that refusal or consent to the visits and interviews would not influence the teacher's treatment of or attitudes toward their child. They also emphasized that they were not inspectors, that they would not carry back any information to the schools, and that they were in no position to help the child in school. Nevertheless, it is possible that some of the parents thought the visits would in some way help their children or, being unclear about the role of the researcher, were afraid not to cooperate. In any event, none of the black parents refused to participate and only one of the white middle-class families declined to become a part of the study.

During the first home visit, all of the researchers had similar general questions to ask the parents in conversational form, having previously committed the interview schedule to memory. In subsequent visits, no formal guidelines for interviews were followed since the main focus of the research was on parent-child interaction, not on interviews by the researchers. The record of home observations included everything the researcher could remember from the time of arrival until the time of departure—ranging from a description of the condition of the neighborhood and the house or apartment building to a chronicle of what was said and done by everyone present in the home during the visit.

During these home visits, researchers dressed casually, were relatively informal, and rarely took notes. As soon as possible after the visit, the researchers dictated an account of what had happened, making verbatim records of what had been said and done to the best of their abilities. In certain instances, they took notes on answers to some specific formal questions but only when they felt that this would not upset the parents or negatively influence their relationships with the family and the effectiveness of their observations.

At different times during the lifetime of the project, the research staff interviewed other classroom teachers, principals, and such staff members as librarians, special teachers, and counselors as well as some higher administrative officers, including the district superintendent, the superintendent, and several members of the school board. Over the three years of the project, the field staff conducted some 75 interviews with teachers and other school personnel. The staff attended and dictated accounts of 11 teachers' meetings and 11 PTA meetings. They also made detailed notes on informal conversations with teachers and principals in the lounges and in the halls, and with children in the halls, on the playgrounds, and on field trips. Additional sources of data included report cards, samples of classroom materials and assignments, office memos to the teachers, and children's drawings. Periodically, they drew diagrams of the seating arrangements of the classes. In all, 316 classroom observations lasting about an hour and a half each were made by the field staff—242 in black classrooms, 74 in white. This amounted to 207 sessions in seven kindergartens, 86 in seven first-grade classrooms, and 23 in one second-grade classroom. Additional observations were conducted in a Head Start program and in two summer-school classrooms where some of the children attended the summer session between kindergarten and first grade.

As soon as possible following each observational period or interview, the field workers dictated protocols of what had occurred onto tapes from their handwritten notes or, in the case of home visits, from memory. These tapes were subsequently transcribed and checked by the researchers. In one school, some material was taped in the classrooms.

A number of different coding schemes were used during the course of the research, including Jules Henry's own scheme described in his article, "A Cross-Cultural Outline of Education."[9] As the research progressed, however, different substantive interests of the staff eventually led to different modes of analyses with the result that no one particular scheme of coding was applied to all of the data.[10]

Selective Perception and Distortion

The limitations of this type of research—with its emphasis on naturalistic or systematic nonparticipant observation—are well known. Among these are not only the very human tendency to be selective about what is seen and not seen but also the danger of subsequently distorting the observations and interpreting them to fit preconceived ideas. Another limitation is the possibility that important kinds of behavior and patterns of activity are missed because the observations are made periodically, not constantly. An additional weakness of the methodology is that replication of the research is impossible. Although similar studies might be done, it would be very difficult to make an exact comparison with the first one. Of course, the time, the actors, and the circumstances would have changed. The point of replication, however, is to test how faithfully a piece of research represents a set of human behaviors or a social situation. Another longitudinal study of the natural history of the experience of black children in elementary school might well interpret the data from quite a different perspective.

Of the possible kinds of selective perception and distortion in the study of the elementary school pupils and their teachers and families, the biases resulting from the differences in the race and class of the observers and the observed were the most worrisome. Most, though certainly not all, of the children and their families were both poor and black. In contrast, the field staff, male and female, were all middle class by virtue of both education and occupation, and seven out of nine were white. All of the research directors were also middle class and white. Although the project was alert to the biases, prejudices, and stereotypes stemming from these class and racial differences and even though there was a conscious attempt to keep such biases from distorting the findings, there was no means of knowing how well selective perception and distortion were controlled.

There was another situation which was important for some of the research outcomes, yet impossible to control and difficult to assess. This had to do with reactions of the children's parents to being visited in their homes by the research team. What were the families' perceptions of the researchers? Were they seen as officials in disguise who might do some harm? Were they afraid that the researchers might have something to do with cutting off relief, bringing down the wrath of the school on their child, or negatively evaluating some family activity? There is little doubt that some of the parents were highly suspicious of the researchers and protected themselves in various ways, such as by agreeing with every statement made by a researcher, never volunteering information, pretending lack of understanding, or praising, feeding, and joking with the researcher. Sensing their mothers' fears, the children may also have been on guard against the researchers' intrusions. The intention of a parent to manipulate the observer by making expected rather than candid responses was evident. The following is a report of a conversation between a researcher and Mrs. Green, Billy's mother:

Mrs. Green looks very much interested while the researcher explains why he is observing in Billy's classroom at school. She constantly agrees with his statements about school, "That's right . . . Parents got to be interested in their children." "Education's really important these days. . . . I see what you means; I know that school is important." "I see, I know it's important what the child learns." (Researcher notes that Mrs. Green has not visited the school, does not attend PTA meetings, Open House and does not know where Billy's report card is.)[11]

Mrs. Green's handling of the researcher was typical of the way in which one group of parents and teachers reacted to the presence of the field staff in their classrooms and homes. Others reacted quite differently. Generally, they seemed to represent four types of responses to the experience of being included in the study: status seekers, service demanders, unbelievers, and passive accepters.[12]

Status Seekers

The status seekers viewed their association with a university research project as a personal compliment and as a possible means of enhancing their position in their private social circles, among their co-workers, and even in the community at large. They were not only very cooperative with the researchers in doing whatever they were asked but they tried to become friends with the interviewers. Intimacy-seeking behavior was common. Among the parents, it was not surprising that the so-called status seekers were predominantly the parents of those children whom the teachers had chosen as being potentially successful in school. These parents reacted very positively to being included in the research and sought to extend the relationship with the researchers beyond the demands of the project itself. A visit with a middle-class black family was illustrative of this:

Mrs. Deveraux went into the kitchen and fixed the researcher a drink, a rather mild one, and then came back into the living room and sat down. At this point the grandmother asked the researcher when he was going to bring his wife by so that they could meet her. The researcher didn't have a chance to answer the question before Mrs. Deveraux said that she was thinking of holding a small tea when Mrs. Johnson (the child's teacher), the researcher and his wife, and she and her husband and the grandmother could all get together and simply chat. She said that she was very anxious to meet the researcher's wife and that this might be a rather informal and pleasant way of doing it.[13]

Similarly, the principals of the two white suburban schools behaved as if the presence of university researchers in their schools was a status verification for them. They seemed to assume that their schools had been selected for inclusion in the study because of their schools' outstanding success in producing students with records of very high achievement. They were very ready to talk about their own schools and laud them as being exemplary. They also shared confidences with the research staff in the form of descriptions of their adroitness at manipulating the parents, children, and teachers in their schools. Among the teachers in these same schools, there was some sense that having an observer in their classrooms was a feather in their caps, but the strain of being watched sometimes turned the compliment into a mixed blessing.

Service Demanders

Having the same observers in their classrooms throughout the year created a situation in which it was natural for the teachers to draw the outsiders into a closer, more personal relationship. Some teachers treated the researchers as confidantes, sharing with them frustrations and misgivings connected with their work and letting them know that they were grateful for someone to talk to about their problems. They sometimes even apologized for how they conducted their classrooms as if to ward off criticism by the researchers. This did not mean that they readily admitted any deficiencies in themselves as teachers. What they did was to complain about the shortcomings of their students and working conditions at their schools. Some attempted to involve the research staff in helping them with their work, even to the extent of asking the observers to take on the teaching of a class for a while.

Some of the parents and relatives of the children who were earning low wages or on welfare tried to extend the roles of the researchers beyond the visiting and interviewing which had been agreed to at the outset. In these families the researcher from the university was seen as a possible means of gaining access to resources which the poor parents did not have. The researcher was recognized as someone "too good to go to waste." Services and goods were solicited from them. One researcher become involved in painting a room and fixing a door. Another brought food and books for the children and took them for rides. A third read to the children and helped them with their lessons:

One time one of the older boys, James, burst into the kitchen when the researcher was helping three of the children with their school subjects. Mrs. Green spoke to him, in a very harsh voice. "Boy, shut up while he's teachin' those kids or I'll whup you." She threatened the other children with a whipping, too, especially the youngest, Averell, who kept on laughing. She said that if Averell didn't shut up while they were learning, that she was going to shup 'em. She made a number of verbal threats to the other children to keep quiet and keep out of the way while the researcher and the three children worked on their numbers and ABC's.[14]

Caught in a situation of wanting desperately to ingratiate themselves yet not wanting to become beneficent do-gooders, the researchers had to tread a delicate line between being helpfully responsive and being completely taken over by the subjects of their study. Sooner or later they had to refuse the pleas of their families for the goods and services that these people needed so badly.

Unbelievers

Outright suspicion and hostility were other reactions of the adults who were included in the study. These were the openly unbelieving. They frequently expressed doubt about the researchers' motives for being there and making the study. Some probably feared that the observers were looking for the personal weaknesses of a parent or teacher. One of the teachers was under some pressure from her principal to adopt some changes in the curriculum. Her anxiety about this was unwittingly increased by the presence of an observer in her classroom, since she suspected that the principal had placed an outsider in her room to obtain information about her teaching methods which would then be reported back. She was reduced to tears when she thought she had to teach in front of a member of the field staff whom she perceived as a dangerous critic and tale carrier.

Other teachers, while not necessarily suspicious of some unknown purpose of the research project, were doubtful as to whether the field staff would be in their classrooms long enough to understand their instructional programs and to see how the children progressed. In addition, some of the teachers felt that the observers were more interested in their mistakes than their successes. One day during naptime when a white suburban teacher was surprised by having a researcher walk into her room unannounced while she was admonishing a child rather severely, she became obviously quite flustered. But the real fear of being observed in a disapproved act was connected with hitting and spanking the children. In one suburban classroom when a teacher tapped a child on his buttocks, she looked at the researcher and said ruefully, "Write that down in your little book." Her tone and expression indicated that this was the last thing she wanted the researcher to do.

Once when an observer unexpectedly entered a first-grade classroom in a ghetto school, the teacher suddenly stopped what she was doing as the door opened. She was still in the act of leaning over a child who was crying and the entire class was funereally silent. The teacher said very abruptly, "That's all," and the child want back to her seat. However, not all of the teachers were careful about not being observed striking the children—only one took the precaution of using the cloakroom out of sight of the researchers.

Some of the teachers in the ghetto schools felt that the field staff was there to write another of "those" books condemning ghetto schools, and they were opposed to having the research carried on in their classrooms. "What are you going to do to really help these children and not just help yourself?" a teacher asked. The strongest resistance came from a young black teacher in a federally funded Room of Twenty. Although she had observers and apprentice teachers in her room continually, she was fearful of having the white researchers because she thought they would not understand the black children's positive attributes and assumed that they would also be critical of the teaching methods used by the black teachers. She accused the researchers of being soft on the children and of not appreciating why the teachers needed to be strict disciplinarians.

Passive Accepters

The fourth, but far from the smallest, category of adults under observation was made up of passive accepters. These were those teachers and parents who might not have wanted the field staff in their classrooms and homes but did not deny them entry. The teachers in the ghetto schools lacked the prerogative of refusal since permission to have observers in their classrooms had come from the school superintendent. In the middle-class schools, on the other hand, the teachers were allowed to decide whether the observers should be admitted to their classrooms. As for the parents, only one middle-class white parent refused to be a part of the research. None of the black parents turned down the interviewers' requests to be regular visitors in their homes.

So the passive accepters consisted of the poor black parents and most of their children's teachers. The parents had learned through past experience to tolerate the intrusions of public and private governmental agencies, particularly the welfare department, into their intimate lives. Although they may have feared reprisals against their children in school, some of the parents made a practice of avoiding the researchers whenever possible, even though they had consented to the visits. One strategy was simply not being at home at the time of the visit. Another tactic was making the researchers feel uncomfortable by not paying much attention to them when they made their visits. Most of the time, though, the mothers of the children received the researchers in a passive but civil way and went on pretty much with what they had been doing —cooking, watching television, sleeping—after having exchanged the usual amenities with the researchers when they showed up once a week to call on the families.

One member of the research staff became convinced that the black families usually hid their real beliefs and attitudes from the observers. As she put it:

It might be asked whether the majority of descriptions of black parents and children are anything more than descriptions of the black families' adaptation to the presence of a white middle-class professional, a condescending interviewer, or an unenlightened do-gooder.

One can ask what in a black child's past experience with members of the white majority would motivate him to vulnerability and expression of his inner feelings: also why should a black mother, already experienced with the welfare office and the police department, have any trust in a researcher who visits once or twice a week? The answer is of course that there is little reason for trust or sharing of confidences and there is a great likelihood of obtaining of information which only serves to support the already existing stereotypes of the ghetto family.

No one should assume for a moment that black persons are naive concerning their position in society nor the motivation of most researchers. Futhermore, they are quite adept at playing games with the researcher and managing to hide their attitudes.[15]

Because of these difficulties relating to quality of the data on family interaction, the research staff was particularly cautious about making interpretations based on their home observations. On the other hand, they found that the youngsters behaved pretty consistently in the way they related to their parents and teachers during the several years that the field staff visited their homes and classrooms. Being too young and unsophisticated to understand what a research project wanted with their lives, the children did not appear to alter their behavior when they were around the research staff. During school hours, they acted either shy or friendly or simply ignored the fact that they had regular visitors in their classrooms. In their homes the children usually sat around in silence for a while at the beginning of a researcher's visit and then roughhoused among themselves or slipped out of sight to continue playing. At their mothers' prodding to say something polite to a guest, the children occasionally talked to the researchers and, when they were better acquainted, tried to involve the visitors in their play. Quite often the youngsters devised ingenious ways of persuading staff members to give them something they wanted, such as food or money.

Such attempts to include the observers in activities with the children was a problem to the research staff because, as nonparticipant observers, they did not wish to become a regular part of the interaction. As much as the observers tried to remain apart, some of the teachers did not permit them to do this. One teacher regularly used an observer as a convenient disciplinary agent. She would chastise certain children for misbehaving while they were "having company." At other times she would say that the students were being granted a stay of punishment because "company" was in the room. One researcher felt that he was sometimes being used as a substitute for the principal who would ordinarily have been chosen by the teacher to play the role of imminent punisher.

The possibility that the teachers changed the way they taught their lessons and treated their pupils while they were being observed was not ignored. It could be argued that if a teacher modified her behavior in the presence of outsiders, it would have been in the direction of attempting to live up to her conception of how an ideal teacher would conduct her class. As a professional, she would try to do her best teaching, not her poorest, while being observed. One check on observer effect on teacher behavior was the fact that some of the teachers were observed by more than one member of the research team. When several observers saw a teacher act consistently over a two-year period, for example, they had more reason to feel that they had a good sample of that teacher's interaction with her pupils.

Possibly, the project made more accurate records of the children's ordinary behavior at school than at home. However, it must be said that being acquainted with many of the children over a period of several years gave the researchers a good deal of confidence about the soundness and depth of their knowledge of children's normal ways of behaving both at home and at school. Patricia and Reginald and their classmates were distinct and recognizable individuals as they pursued their careers as pupils learning success or failure in their first three years of schooling and as they grew from being five years old to seven years old at home.

Notes

1. Carol S. Talbert, "The Weeding-Out Process: The Relation Between Black American English and Educational Achievement," mimeographed, 1972. Material on Mrs. Bobb's class was adapted from pp. 36-41.

2. Vera P. John, "The Intellectual Development of Slum Children: Some Preliminary Findings," *American Journal of Orthopsychiatry,* 33 (1963), pp. 813-22; and Martin Deutsch, "The Role of Social Class in Language Development and Cognition" (prepared for the Institute for Developmental Studies, Department of Psychiatry, New York Medical College, April 1964).

3. Kenneth B. Clark, *Dark Ghetto* (New York: Harper and Row, 1965), pp. 129ff.

4. Arthur Pearl, "Schools Versus Kids," in Irwin Deutscher and Elizabeth J. Thompson, eds., *Among the People: Encounters with the Poor* (New York: Basic Books, 1968), p. 162.

5. Helen P. Gouldner with the assistance of John Bennett, Marshall Durbin, Ray C. Rist, and Carol S. Talbert (Jules Henry, former principal investigator), "The Natural History of the Education of the Black Child in the City" (final report to the Bureau of Research, Office of Education, U.S. Department of Health, Education and Welfare, project no. 6-2771, June 1971).

6. Jules Henry, *Culture Against Man* (New York: Random House, 1963).

7. As is often the case, focuses different from those originally anticipated emerged as the research proceeded. Thus, for example, some emphasis was placed on the structure, philosophy, and problems of the school system. In addition, several substudies in linguistics were done, including one on the use of Black American English in classroom teaching and another on the lexical differentiation between children in kindergarten and those in the sixth and eighth grades. See Marshall Durbin, "The Position of Black English in the English Language" (paper presented to the Department of Speech and Hearing Pathology, Southern Illinois University, February 1970); "An Essay on Black American English," chapter 4 in Gouldner, "The Natural History of the Education of the Black Child"; Carol S. Talbert, "Socio-Linguistic Analysis of Teachers and Pupils" (paper delivered at the annual meeting of the American Anthropological Association, November 1969); "A Socio-Linguistic Analysis of Classroom Ecology" (paper presented at the American Educational Research Association Symposium, March 1970); "The Implications of Spoken Black English Upon Strategies in the Classroom and in the Social Sciences" (paper presented at the annual meeting of the American Orthopsychiatric Association, March 1970).

8. Carol S. Talbert, unpublished protocol.

9. Jules Henry, "A Cross-Cultural Outline of Education," *Current Anthropology* 1 (July 1960), pp. 267-305.

10. It should be noted that all the school personnel involved in the research were fully informed about the nature of the project and were guaranteed anonymity. No classroom was observed without first securing the consent of the principal. No classroom materials, such as children's homework or tests, were taken without the teacher's consent. Both the teachers and principals, as well as the assistant superintendent, had the last word in deciding which materials would be used. If the teachers and school officials were hesitant about furnishing materials requested, no pressure was placed upon them. Although real names, except for teachers and principals, were employed in typed protocols, code names for all subjects were used in all published and unpublished papers. Code names were also used for the schools, street names, and all locations in which research was undertaken. Protocols were kept in a locked file accessible only to the project staff. A clear and honest representation of the project's purpose was made to each of the families observed, although they were not told why their children had been chosen. No account of the activities taking place in the homes of the children was carried back to school personnel.

11. Marco M. Pardi, unpublished protocol.

12. Talbert, "The Weeding-Out Process." The material on the typology of adult subjects is adapted from pp. 7-11. However, the Talbert typology does not include the service demanders as a separate type.

13. Talbert, "The Weeding-Out Process." p. 8 (from an unpublished protocol of Marco M. Pardi).

14. Talbert, "The Weeding-Out Process," p. 9 (from an unpublished protocol of Marco M. Pardi).

15. Carol S. Talbert, "A Discussion of Research Aims and Strategies for Studying Inner-City Family Behavior" (paper presented at the annual meeting of the American Educational Research Association, March 1970), p. 2.

CHAPTER 2 Settling Down

Kindergarten was the first school experience of most of the five-year-old children in the four all-black schools in which observations were made by the research team. With only a few exceptions, the children had not attended a preschool of any kind before entering kindergarten, but on opening day the youngsters immediately found out how they were expected to behave. The teachers made it clear to their new pupils that they wanted them to be quiet and obedient, and to follow directions carefully. In most cases, the children learned to comply with their teachers' wishes very quickly, especially with the rule about not being noisy. By early in September the youngsters had already settled down to being remarkably quiet. When members of the research team rated the noise level in the classrooms—and they did this every 15 minutes, using a 5-point scale in which 0 equaled silence, 1 equaled some noise, 2 was more active buzzing, 3 was quite noisy, and 4 indicated chaos—they found that the noise level rarely rose above 1 on the scale. The teachers seemed to possess an exquisite sensitivity to sound, so much so that they frequently reproved a child for speaking when an observer sitting quite close by had not heard him say anything. The various techniques which were used by the teachers to keep the noise level so low were described by Jules Henry:

Teachers have different ways of enforcing silence, order, and obedience. One may walk around the room in constant vigilance; another may rely more on verbal admonitions or on paralinguistic devices like stares or sharp tones. Sometimes children are hit.

The sound level had been so reduced by control techniques that, although we wanted to record the children's conversations . . . it was very difficult to pick up child speech in the classroom.[1]

Knowing the tendency for American school children to be unruly, the field staff had expected to see much of the teachers' energies devoted to keeping order.[2] What they had not expected was the teachers' insistence on almost total silence in the classrooms and halls—and their success at achieving it. In fact, during the weekly seminars of the research project, all the observers reported independently upon what they felt was an eerie stillness prevailing throughout the school buildings they visited. They decided to talk this over with the teachers and the other school staff while they were discussing methods and philosophies of teaching during their informal conversations and structured interviews.

The teachers, it was found, were in total agreement on the necessity for silence in the classrooms and halls and for tight control over the children. In their opinion, the ideal setting for learning was a quiet, orderly classroom where there was "a place for everything and everything was in its place," where no one spoke without permission, and where interaction was only between teacher and pupil. A good class had children who had learned to sit quietly at their desks, raise their hands before talking, wait patiently for the bell to ring before leaving their seats, stand in line with their partners in an orderly way, and when in school repress any expression of anger, frustration, or exuberance. The teachers strove to reach this ideal, and some of them achieved it. Those teachers who had reputations for running a tight ship were greatly respected by their colleagues and the principal. Indeed, a teacher seemed to be judged more often by whether she was a good disciplinarian than by any other standard such as the academic performance of her pupils.

During conversations with the field staff about teaching and other topics, the teachers frequently brought up the subjects of discipline and control of their own accord. These problems seemed to be uppermost in their minds—a preoccupation usually expressed as a need to "keep the kids in line." The teachers were greatly worried about whether or not they would be able to control their classes. Several explained that their choice to teach a particular class was determined first and foremost by whether they could "stay on top of the class . . . . The children will run all over you if they think they're big enough to get away with it."

A number of the experienced teachers had repeatedly told their principals that they would refuse to take a room beyond a certain grade level. Although there was no consensus about the cutoff point separating manageable and unmanageable age groups, each teacher had a definite opinion which applied to what she herself would be willing to undertake. A few stated that they would not teach any class beyond the second grade; one chose the fifth as her top limit; another said she was willing to take any class but the eighth grade. Obviously, the very young children in kindergarten and the first and second grades did not offer the same challenge to teacher control which was presented by the older, stronger, more rebellious pupils in the upper grades of the elementary school. Even so, the teachers did not alter their notions about the strict discipline needed in the lower grades, even though the little ones were easier to manage.

Fear was one of the ingredients of the teachers' anxieties about managing their classes. Some apprentice teachers had really dreaded being left alone in a classroom until they were sure that they had the skills to keep the students under control. Though most of the teachers of the younger children did not elaborate on the source of their fears, their insistence on silence and absolute order seemed to stem from beliefs which they held about the dire consequences of any relaxation of an iron-handed rule. These beliefs were, first, that if the children were given any latitude at all in their behavior, the classroom would rapidly become chaotic and the children would be unable to concentrate on learning. Second, once a teacher had lost the ability to keep a room absolutely quiet and orderly, the chaos that would follow would be succeeded in quick order by violence. "The older children would just as soon hit you as look at you" was the way it was put.

The assumptions about human behavior and learning underlying this causal chain of events were taken for granted as truisms and acted upon by all of the teachers as a basis for conducting their classrooms. Although there are many approaches other than harsh discipline which are used by American teachers to maintain order and create a context for learning, the teachers in these schools had made up their minds about what worked best in their classrooms notwithstanding their familiarity with other methods which they may have studied in courses on child development and learning theory. In fact, from conversations with the teachers, it was evident that their justifications for using tight control in the classroom were formulated less often in terms of whether it made for good teaching than whether it resulted in less trouble for themselves.

The general atmosphere in the classrooms being observed was not only quiet and orderly, but harsh. Of course, each teacher had her own style of conducting her class. There were differences in how "authoritarian," at one extreme, or "democratic," at the other, the teachers were in the management of their pupils. They were all fairly authoritarian. There were teachers whom the field staff saw meting out physical punishment. It was not unusual to see a teacher shaking a child, pushing his head down on the desk, and pulling at his arm. However, actual beatings were relatively rare and, as noted in the following episode in a kindergarten class, corporal punishment was usually administered out of sight of the rest of the children, at least when an observer was present:

During the music lessons, some of the children had been singing out of tune or had been singing the wrong words at the wrong times. The teacher came back to her desk and said irritatedly, "You know what, boys and girls? We'll have to stop for a minute, for some of you think it's time to play." She called up three boys and one girl to the front of the room and said flatly, "Some of our friends, come over here." They came to her desk and she picked up a stick. It was about 14 inches long, round and looked like bamboo. One at a time the teacher took the four children into the cloakroom and hit them. I could not see the actual beating, but I could count the number of times the stick made contact. Harold was first and she struck him 20 times; Ben was second and she hit him 14 times; Lynda was hit 14 times and Bobby caught it 12 times. Each kid began to cry even before he was hit, and each cried during the whipping and after. The children at their seats were all staring at the cloakroom with somber expressions on their faces, but there was no sound out of them. When Lynda was in the cloakroom I could hear the teacher say, softly, "Bend way over." The whipping took place between 9:28 and 9:30 a.m.

The teacher made short work of them and the children went back to their seats crying, and she went back to the record player. Then the whole class sang, "The Ding-Dong Choo Choo" in a very somber tone. This time when they got through the song, there were no smiles.[3]

The teachers used bodily contact with the students more often as a means of control than as an expression of encouragement or affection. No doubt such physical contact with the teacher influenced how secure, relaxed, and accepted the children felt during their first years of schooling. "When American children display behaviors indicating their feeling of social closeness to the teacher," Jules Henry has hypothesized, "the teacher will probably be found to be 'integrative.' He will show pleasure at correct responses, occasionally pat a child, be encouraging, move about the room, let them come close to him."[4] Such behavior was not generally engaged in by the kindergarten and first-grade teachers in the ghetto schools being observed. True, the teachers patted and hugged a few of the children who were their favorites, but for the rest they frequently used bodily contact to hurt a child physically as a means of forcing him to behave properly. On the other hand, bodily contact was almost never used to console a child who was upset. A typical episode occurred during a music period in a kindergarten:

Mrs. Short is teaching the class a new song for Thanksgiving. "Let's go over the words again for the Turkey Song." The children repeat the words twice and then sing the song. However, most of them still don't seem to know it.

At the end of the first trial, Pamela starts crying and immediately Mrs. Ad, the classroom teacher, says, "Wilbur, move back a little bit. Billy Fisk, you move over here." Hearing this, Mrs. Short speaks softly to herself, "I don't really think that's the reason." (She seems to be referring to the fact that Mrs. Ad moved Wilbur and Billy as if they had caused Pamela to cry.) Mrs. Short then asks rather calmly, "What's wrong, Pamela?" Pamela does not reply.

Mrs. Short addresses the whole class again, "Is there anybody who thinks they can sing by themselves?" The children—mostly the girls, and three or four boys—raise their hands. Mrs. Short calls on Ginny and Juanita who go up to the front of the room to sing. Neither one of them seems to know the words very well, but the teacher sings along with them and, at the end of the song, says, "That was pretty good," and the girls return to their seats.

Pamela is still crying and Mrs. Ad moves over toward her saying, "Pamela, we can't hear the song for you." Mrs. Short continues with the lesson, "Let's try some of the boys." Many of the boys raise their hands and she calls on Frank, Irving, David and Lee. The four boys come to the front of the room and Mrs. Short starts playing the song again on the piano. Three of them mumble the words, but Frank just stands looking at the door, distracted by a girl who comes into the room bringing a note to the teacher. Mrs. Short stops playing and says, "All right, let's begin . . . come on, there's four of you," and she starts from the beginning again. Irving and Frank seem to know most of the words, but none of the boys know them all very well.

At the end of the song, Mrs. Ad says, "Pamela, we can't have our lesson if you keep disturbing us. You'll have to be quiet." When Pamela cries even louder, Mrs. Ad speaks to her in a very irritated tone, "Shh, you'll have to shut up," but Pamela continues to cry.

Mrs. Short calls on Emily, Pat, Carol and Dorothy who go to the front of the room. They sing the song very well, albeit out of tune like the other two groups. At the end Mrs. Short compliments the girls, saying, "That was good." Pamela is still crying. Ignoring the distraction caused by Pamela's crying, Mrs. Short continues the music lesson, "This morning, we're going to learn a song about Indian warriors." Pamela cries even louder, whereupon Mrs. Ad gets up and declares loudly, "We can't have this," and grabs Pamela rather forcefully by the arm, pushing her into the cloakroom. Pamela offers some resistance, but Mrs. Ad keeps pushing her. When they reach the door, Mrs. Ad shakes her rather violently and talks to her.

It is about an hour before recess. Pamela stays isolated in the cloakroom. When she stops crying for a short while, no one takes any notice. She starts crying again. When the bell rings for recess, the teacher goes into the cloakroom and tries to force Pamela to put on her coat and go outside, but Pamela refuses to do this. She falls to the floor and cries harder. The teacher leaves her there and accompanies the other children to the stairs.[5]

The field staff made note of many occurrences of this kind of treatment by the teachers. The findings of their studies of the consequences of these teaching techniques for the behavior and progress in schoolwork of the children are discussed later. As has already been mentioned, the field staff also made observations in several suburban all-white elementary schools and in a school situated in a blue-collar neighborhood in a relatively small industrial city. This allowed for comparisons in the ways the teachers conducted their classes and handled the children in three types of school populations. For example, an observer witnessed a crying incident in a suburban kindergarten where the teacher treated a child in distress very differently from the way Pamela was dealt with in the incident just described:

Mrs. Honey is singing quietly, using hand motions along with the tune. The song is about a turtle and is faster than the one sung before. John begins to cry. One of the girls volunteers, "I know that song." John's crying becomes louder. Suddenly the door of the classroom is filled with running and shouting children from one of the higher grades. The teacher looks at John and says, "Those are some children out to play from the big school." The song about the turtle begins again . . . . John cries. "We don't cry," says the teacher and puts her hand on his leg . . . then returns to face the class.

"We have had three songs about a rabbit, a little turtle and a balloon." The teacher continues, "We have 11 kinds of wonderful things to play with." She addresses herself to John, "Sweetheart, come here. Go back and dry your eyes." She gives him a Kleenex and he goes back and sits down wiping his eyes. She says, in a very mock quiet voice, "Whisper, whisper." John is still sniffling.

The teacher now rises from her chair and walks to the front of the classroom. She begins to point at the wall on which there are ten large pictures of people in various poses and asks, "What do you suppose they're doing?" John interrupts again amid his tears and asks for something. Addressing herself to the entire class, Mrs. Honey explains, "We have two fountains and we don't get up just any time."

John begins to hold his mouth, puts his head down and Mrs. Honey, in a small flurry of activity, points to the bathroom. The child runs and makes loud vomiting noises. Mrs. Honey rushes to him. The children have all remained in their chairs though they wiggle and talk among themselves about

John going to the bathroom . . . and there is some giggling. The teacher does not stay in the bathroom with John but returns to the classroom and says to them, "That's why it is a good idea to stop crying because you can get sick. Luckily he told me before it was too late and he'll be back soon." One of the boys in the class said, "He ought to go outside and play." The teacher ignores this. She says to John in the bathroom, "John, are you ready to come back? You just didn't feel so hot, did you?" The teacher goes into the bathroom and flushes the toilet again. John comes out and stands over by the sink which is on one side of the room. The teacher says, "You're all better now. Go back to your seat."[6]

Unlike the teacher in the ghetto school, this teacher first spoke sympathetically to a child who was disturbing the class by his crying and then used bodily contact as a means of comforting him when he was upset and subsequently ill. In the kindergarten in the working-class school in the small city, however, the teacher neither comforted a child who was crying nor punished him physically. Instead she taunted him verbally when he acted shy:

Once again, table by table, the children are instructed to come to the blackboard which is behind the teacher's desk in front of the room. One little boy remains seated at his table, his hands to his eyes, and does not come to the blackboard. Miss June says, "Henry, come to the blackboard." Pause. "OK, go ahead and cry, Henry, I think it would be nice if our guest (the observer) could see you cry." Then Miss June turns to me. I am seated in the back of the room, and she says loudly, "Henry doesn't like to do anything academic. It's that way with the kids in this family all the way up to the 6th grade. We don't know what to do." By this time, Henry has walked up and taken a seat on the floor in the back row of the semicircle. His head is bowed and he is rubbing his eyes. Many of the children look at Henry or look at me. I do not respond.[7]

Henry's crying was not allowed to escape the attention of his peers or of the visiting observer. Rather, it was specifically mentioned and the inference was made publicly that there was something wrong with his family, that they were crybabies and nonlearners.

In the three types of schools observed the teachers frequently used bodily contact as a way of controlling a child who was overly active. During the rest period in kindergarten when the children are expected to lie down or sit at their desks, close their eyes, and even take a nap, teachers often have to quiet the children who do not want to make the shift from activity to repose. The following incident took place in a ghetto kindergarten during a rest period in which the children had been instructed to put their heads down on their desks and close their eyes:

One of the boys is out of his desk sliding on the floor. The teacher grabs him by the arm and says in a harsh tone, "Sit down, sit down right here. Put your head down." Then she pushes the boy's head down on the desk roughly.[8]

One of the field staff reported a contrasting mode of control employed in a suburban kindergarten during a rest period. In this instance, kindly rather than harsh bodily contact was used as a subtler means of inhibiting and restraining an active child:

The children are lying on small mats on the floor. Thomas is singing to himself. The teacher says, "Thomas, do you remember? Come here just a minute." Thomas crawls slowly and then duckwalks over to the teacher. She whispers to him, "You don't want to go back to my old office again," and she makes a face. He grins and sort of looks at her. She puts her arm around him and holds him tight up against her leg. He lies down again. Paul is trying to call John Simpson. The teacher says, "No, Paul, John doesn't want to talk to you now . . . ." All of the children are resting now and Mrs. Honey walks over to the researcher to talk.[9]

In one of the ghetto schools observed by Carol Talbert, there was no letup in the strict, punitive treatment of the children by the teachers, even when they supervised the playground:

During recess all the school is on the playground at the same time. On one typical day the kindergarten teacher happens to be yard monitor. She is carrying a 4-foot rattan cane which all the teachers have. As the researcher talks with her, four children approach. The teacher threatens them, tapping her cane on the blacktop, making a harsh clicking sound.

There is a lot of running, playing and roughhousing on the playground. The girls play jump rope with rubber bands strung together. There are no organized games—the volleyball nets are used only to swing on. The gym teacher stands to the side of the yard, periodically shouting a directive to someone near.

The bell rings at 10:20. The children scream much louder than before, and all turn around and run toward the back of the building where the lines are formed before entering the building. Mrs. Sterling, a yard monitor, walks along the lines snapping the stick on the ground yelling, "Get in line there, boy! You don't play in line!" She walks back and forth along several lines, aiming the stick directly behind the heels of the children. They bend backward as though anticipating actual bodily contact. Another teacher threatens, "You gonna get it upstairs, boy!" Several of the little boys make the motions of shooting a gun at some pigeons flying by overhead. The second bell rings and the lines begin to move through the doorway into the school, with the teachers bringing up the rear.[10]

In sharp contrast with this drill-sergeant behavior, the teachers in the upper-middle-class schools acted as if they were almost afraid of hurting a young child's feelings. They seemed to think that a child's self-image was fragile, and consequently talked and behaved as if no action taken by themselves or by any child in a classroom was irrelevant if it might result in some harm to another child's feelings about himself. The teachers in the ghetto classrooms, on the other hand, often behaved as if they and the students were antagonistic forces. For example, they routinely turned down offers of children who volunteered to recite. In addition, they made a habit of putting many of the children in the position of failing to give the correct answer when called upon to recite, as can be seen in the following episode:

"Now, who knows the number for today?" Lee, who is still standing following an earlier recitation says, "Twenty-eight," to which Mrs. Short replies, "You told us one thing already, Lee." Aron raises his hand and says "Twenty-seven." Mrs. Short replies to Aron, "No, twenty-seven was yesterday. What number comes after twenty-seven?" Aron tries six. "No, Aron. What comes after twenty-seven, Claude?" "Eighteen" is Claude's answer. "No. Claude. Pamela, do you know?" Pamela shakes her head. "Paula, do you know?" Paula tries, "Twenty-six." "No, Tuesday was the twenty-sixth. What is the number, Diane?" Diane says, "Twenty-eight." "Yes, Diane, it is twenty-eight." Diane gets the number from the desk and puts it on the calendar.[11]

Another teacher made a practice of refusing to allow certain children to participate whenever they offered to help in some way:

"Rose, go and get the beads for your table. Kim, get the beads for your table. Alice, you get the beads for yours." Stephen waves his hand and asks, "Can I help?" "No, I don't need anybody helping me who can't sit down and who's noisy." Stephen gets up and goes to get some of the boards. "Steve, get in your seat. I didn't tell you to do one thing." Stephen takes the boards to his seat and passes them out to the children at this table.[12]

In a kindergarten in which a speech specialist conducted lessons once a week, the children sitting at the back tables rarely responded to the teacher's questions unless she called on them directly to recite. It was not until the fifth of these sessions that one of the children from the "slower" tables volunteered to give an answer:

John, who has sat passively and quietly throughout the lesson, stands up all of a sudden at the rear of the group and calls to Miss Allen, "Call on me." The tone of his voice is somewhat desperate as he seeks to have the teacher select him for the question. Miss Allen, however, replies, "John, sit down. I cannot call on anyone who shouts in class." John slumps back to the floor and turns his back to the speech teacher. He does not say a word for the rest of the lesson.[13]

Some children who were rarely called on to recite contributed answers spontaneously but were ignored even when the answers were correct:

"Who can tell me the name of the month?" The teacher calls on Carol who stands up and says, "September." The teacher corrects her, "Say, the name of this month is . . . September," and Carol says after her, "The name of this month is September." "Yes, Carol, now who can tell me the name of the season?" A boy hollers out, "Fall." The teacher ignores him, "Everybody raised their hands so nice except you." She then calls on another boy who says, "This season is September."[14]

Byron was the object of scorn of another teacher who was teaching the children a song:

Frank comes up to the front of the room and sings the new song very well. He knows the words and sings them loudly and clearly, although very much out of tune and in a much lower pitch than the song is being played in. When he finishes, the teacher compliments him, "That was nice. Now let's give him three claps." The children clap. "I like the way he sang out loud like that." "Now, Byron, will you come up here, since you were helping everyone else." Byron goes to the front of the room to sing but he does not know many of the words and he sings very softly. When he finishes, the teacher speaks to him very sternly, "You don't even know the words and you were talking. Now you listen and we'll try it again some other time. Learn the words."[15]

In contrast to this, a child in a white upper-middle-class school received immediate support and help from his teacher when he was having difficulty mastering a task:

A boy is struggling to put together the pieces of a wooden puzzle. He starts to shake and screw up his face. The teacher notices this and walks over to him almost immediately. He begins to cry. "Oh, well," says the teacher, "I'll help you put it together. See, it's even hard for me. I can hardly do it. There we go." Another boy who has joined them volunteers, "Well, I put it together right away by myself." The teacher keeps reassuring the first child, "There you are. Good for you." She has helped him put in another piece. "See, we've got it all done. We can't be expected to do all the very hard puzzles on the first day." The boy stops crying and appears satisfied.[16]

Like the other teachers in the suburban school, this teacher gave the children a great deal of individual attention, support, approval, and encouragement. She walked around the room during play periods, for example, touching the children and making comments such as, "That's good" and "If you want to play, go right on." Many times she sat down and worked along with a child or, when children were working together in groups of threes or fours, she encouraged the members of the group to cooperate with each other. Extra individual attention was also given by the teacher to prevent accidents from becoming stressful, as seen in this incident:

About half the children are in the semicircle now. The others are putting things away. One of the two girls who is playing with the snap blocks drops the whole box and the snap blocks go all over the floor again. The teacher goes over and helps her pick them up and put them back in the box, but the teacher doesn't finish the job. She leaves, and the other girls are helping to pick up the rest of them.[17]

In the ghetto school an incident such as this was cause for isolation.

Henry is attempting to put away his pegs; he drops the entire board on the floor. A girl says, "See!" and a few of the children say, "Oooo!" The teacher walks over and for a while has a disturbed expression on her face which she clears up and says, "Now tomorrow, Henry, you won't get to play with the pegs because you don't know what to do with them." Henry looks at the teacher and says nothing and gets down on the floor to pick up the pegs. The other children put their pegs and boards on the shelf. The teacher says, "All my children, come over here and sit on the floor. All but Henry. Henry is gonna stay and pick up pegs."[18]

Isolation of a child from the rest of the class was a disciplinary technique commonly used by all of the teachers, but those in the suburban schools went about it quite differently from the teachers in the all-black schools. If a child was talking with other children and keeping them from concentrating on their work, a teacher might take him gently by the hand and say, "If we are finished early, we'll leave." She would then seat the child in a chair at a distance from the others and hand him a book.[19]

There were many occasions when the teachers in the ghetto schools rejected the mere approach of a child and also simply ignored the children's requests for needed materials:

Howard comes up to Mrs. James' desk to ask her something, but before he has an opportunity to speak, she says in an irritable voice, "Listen, don't come up unless I call you." Another boy speaks up, "Teacher, we need some more," referring to beads. Mrs. James ignores him. Someone else in the room is making the noise, "Choo, choo, choo, choo." The teacher says, "Robert, come up here." When Robert reaches the desk, she asks him, "Is that you making the noise like a train?" Robert shakes his head, indicating that he isn't. "Well, you go and sit down," she says very sternly.[20]

The teachers often appeared not to want to be near the children for reasons that they did not explain to them. The children's advances were turned down arbitrarily:

Wilbur is sitting at his table trying to get the observer's attention, saying things like, "You know my name?" or "I'm gonna hit you." He throws a piece of black crayon and hits the observer, who does not look up. Wilbur walks around in back of the observer and marks the back of his sweater with the crayon and tries to make a mark on his hand. At this point the observer looks up but does not say anything. Wilbur returns to his seat and does not bother the observer anymore, but he gets out of his desk again and goes up to the teacher's desk to say something to her. When he gets very close to her, the teacher says without looking up, "Don't push me while I'm writing."[21]

In the suburban schools a child's legitimate request was immediately and willingly responded to by the teachers:

The little girls sitting around the table making collages are talking, but those who are painting are not talking. All of the other children are talking to each other in quiet voices. One of the girls points to the observer. Another girl says, "You mean that one?" There is no response. Another girls says to nobody in particular, "So, it won't get on me." She is wiping the excess paint onto her smock, saying, "Look at mine now." Another child drops paint on her collage in the wrong place. She looks quickly around, picks up the drop of paint and wipes it under the table. A girl gets up from the collage table and walks over to the teacher who says, "Oh, you're out of glue, sweetheart. I'll get you some more. You wait here."[22]

The field staff recorded many instances of the children in the ghetto schools volunteering ideas that were ignored or rejected by the teachers. For instance, during a speech lesson when the class was discussing animals that live on or around the farm the following incident occurred:

Mrs. Sharp says, "You think we can play a game now? I wonder if you can tell me what I am. You know I want you to raise your hand." Mrs. Sharp then makes the sounds of various animals, pictures of which she has just shown the children. The children guess all of them right, and at the end one little boy asks, "Hey, what about a deer?" Mrs. Sharp replies, "Does a deer live on a farm?'' To which the boy replies, ''No, but he live around the farm.'' Mrs. Sharp then states with finality, ''But we didn't talk about the deer. However, there are a lot of them.''[23]

The commands, the reprimands and threats, the rejection of a child's approach, the undermining of his self-image, the rough handling and corporal punishment, all of which were regularly used by the teachers to maintain order, failed to stop the disapproved behavior of the children during the many months it was practiced in the classrooms being observed. The teachers knew this and they often spoke about the continuing discipline problems which prevented them from being effective because they had to spend so much of their time trying to keep order in the classroom. According to the teachers, it was the students' misbehavior that precipitated the need for discipline and caused the teachers to punish the pupils so severely. The boys and girls were viewed as the provocateurs of disciplinary action, uncooperative and threatening to the teachers' self-respect and safety. For example, Mrs. Pickett, a first-grade teacher, talked about how belligerent some of the pupils in her class were and described the ill effects of the children's classroom behavior on her disposition:

''You know, I have to change my disposition.'' I said to her, ''Change your disposition?'' and she said, ''Yes, I have to change my disposition here.'' She went on to point out that she was a different person at home, noting that she was basically a kind person. She continued, ''Isn't it terrible? I can't whip them all the time. It just doesn't do any good.''

Hearing kindergarten and first-grade children referred to as belligerent and disruptive by their teachers evokes an image of what is ordinarily considered an aggressive, destructive, and even hyperaggressive child, one who ''hits, pursues with intent to hit, snatches, pulls roughly, is abusive, spits, throws things violently, breaks things deliberately, is defiant, incites one child to hit another child, emits loud screams deliberately.''[24] However, the children observed in the primary classrooms very seldom behaved this way either toward one another or toward the teacher. In that case, what kind of acts made it necessary for the teachers to inter-rupt a lesson so as to deal with some misbehavior? A reading of the protocols on observations in Mrs. McAllester's and Mrs. Pickett's classrooms revealed that what most frequently provoked the teachers to use some kind of conduct control were a child's getting out of his seat, wandering around the room, opening drawers, rattling papers, leaning across the table, talking with other children, calling out to get the teacher's attention, turning his head or body toward another person or object, or touching another child. The following episode was typical of the manner in which Mrs. McAllester interrupted the flow of her lesson to reprimand a child:

Mrs. McAllester is talking to the boys and girls about their report cards. At this point she is dwelling on the subject of taking care of wraps. She says, with reference to this subject, as an example, "Does Kim hang his coat up?" And she stares threateningly at Kim as Kim had been looking . . . around the room. He nods his head in the affirmative. Mrs. McAllester, peering at the report card says, "Oh, here's something else that's very important. It's a small picture. It's a little boy sitting down. What do you think he is doing?" One girl calls out, "Readin' a library book." Mrs. McAllester says, "He is helping, not like Kim is doing," as Kim, once again, is looking around the room. The teacher continues, addressing Kim, "I won't see the back of your head if you are listening."

Much of the behavior defined by the teachers as disruptive took place in three particular kinds of situations: when the students were unoccupied, during a transition from one activity to another, and in drawn-out recitation sessions. Instances of this sort occurred during lulls in the progress of work in Mrs. McAllester's class:

Mrs. McAllester is readying the overhead projector and the children are sitting on the floor. Marvin Hamilton has his left hand on Carl. Mrs. McAllester looks up and says rather harshly, "Marvin, you take your hands off that boy and put them in your lap or you'll get in trouble."

At another point, Mrs. McAllester is going through the routine of taking attendance, calling the names of the girls and boys one by one:

Kim Kulver, who is still at his desk, waiting for his name to be called, has opened his desk and is quietly rummaging through it. He has taken a colored picture, which he apparently has drawn, out of the drawer and is looking at it. Mrs. McAllester, looking over toward him, says flatly, "Kim Kulver, leave your picture in the drawer." Kim puts it back in the drawer.

Mrs. McAllester has started to conduct the daily calendar lesson:

Kim Kulver is moving around on the floor where the boys and girls are seated cross-legged in their "listening positions" and Mrs. McAllester says, "Kim, do you have enough room?" and she stares at him . . . threateningly and says, "Well, I will wait until Kim is comfortable. I hope . . . Kim will help, for I might ask him what numerals go in the box (referring to one of the squares on the class calendar)."

A new child has entered the room with her mother and Mrs. McAllester has stopped the lesson to talk with them:

While she is talking to the parent, the children are left at their seats unoccupied. The papers and crayons with which they had been previously working have been collected by Mrs. McAllester. James stands in front of the room next to Mrs. McAllester while she talks with the parent. Then Mrs. McAllester places her hands on James' shoulder, uses both hands to push him into a chair at the side of the room. The teacher then says, "James, I think I'll put you at a table by yourself unless you know how to sit."

It seemed as if almost any act could possibly be perceived by the teacher as disruptive:

Marvin Hamilton has gone over to his table to prepare for the crayon lesson. He has opened his drawer and is now leaning across the table, looking around, not really saying anything. Mrs. McAllester comes over to Marvin and says as she takes him by his arm, looking at him threateningly, "Marvin, you are spoiling your table (other children sit at the same table)." At this point she let him go.

According to observations made in several classrooms, most of the disruptive behavior, as defined by the teacher, was engaged in by just a few of the children in each room. James Watts and Marvin Hamilton, for instance, were frequently dealt with severely for small transgressions:

Mrs. McAllester is conducting the roll-taking exercise where she records on a blackboard the number of boys and girls present and absent. She . . .

walks over to James, who has been talking in a very low tone, and using both of her hands, lifts him up and says to him in a threatening tone, "You are going to be our helper today!" As she finishes saying this, she lets go of him and he sits down.

Marvin is talking in a low tone to Carl while one of the boys is leading the alphabet lesson. Mrs. McAllester, who has gone over to her desk, gets up from her desk, comes over to where the boys and girls are sitting and grabs Marvin with her right hand on his right shoulder and pulls him over to table 2, without ever looking at him.

Almost any activity of these few children was defined as disruptive and responded to with threats and rough handling. However, the behavior of the children punished for disrupting the lessons was not significantly different from that of the children not defined as disruptive. In the following episode James Watts was singled out and called down for doing the same thing the other children had just done:

The boys and girls were seated on the floor unoccupied as Mrs. McAllester talked to the janitor. As he was leaving there was a very loud clap of thunder and most of the boys and girls either jumped up or said, "Ooh!" One girl called out, "God's fightin', devil don't belong up there." James Watts, taking up this cue called out with reference to the devil, "First he was rich and then he got up there," and James pointed towards the sky. Mrs. McAllester, who had gone to the record player at the back of the room, looking towards James, said softly but threateningly, "A couple of my helpers will be in serious trouble today."[25]

Children who were considered disruptive by the teacher were reacted to even for things they had not done, while others appeared to have a license to act without adverse reaction. The children considered disruptive were not always in the act of violating the rules when they were punished. At the same time, not all the violations of the rules were seen as disruptive. An unruly act was not in itself the distinguishing element, but who perpetrated it. The teachers simply labeled some children as disruptive and others not, though their particular acts were more alike than different. In other words, the disruptive behavior was not just something inherent in the students which the teacher encountered and had to suppress. Her attitudes toward individual pupils influenced her perceptions of which students were disruptive and which were not—a very subjective judgment on her part.

Although a good deal of disruptive behavior (as defined by the teachers) took place, the dominant characteristic of the classrooms was overt docility. The children made very few independent suggestions. They rarely made spontaneous contributions of any kind, whether within the context of the lessons or otherwise. There was little humor, little expressiveness. The children rarely approached the teachers physically, possibly because of the rejection that they knew would follow. Most of the children were not allowed to roam around the room and look at the books and pictures or to explore other objects that might arouse their curiosity. By and large, the children complied with the expectations of the institution by remaining quiet and orderly.

Notes

1. Jules Henry, Second Quarterly Progress Report, project no. 6-2771 (submitted to U.S. Office of Education, Basic Studies Branch, Division of Elementary and Secondary Education, Department of Health, Education and Welfare, December 1967), pp. 8-9.

2. Jules Henry, "A Cross-Cultural Outline of Education," *Current Anthropology* 1 (July 1960), pp. 267-324. This article on the formal, conscious aspects of education in nonindustrial and industrial cultures systematized many of the theoretical and factual bases for the research project reported on in this book.

3. Jules Henry, Third Quarterly Progress Report, project no. 6-2771 (submitted to U.S. Office of Education, Basic Studies Branch, Division of Elementary and Secondary Education, Department of Health, Education and Welfare, February 1968), pp. 62-63. Edited version.

4. Jules Henry, "A Cross-Cultural Outline of Education," p. 285.

5. Patricia Roberts, "Satisfaction of Dependency Needs and Conformity," mimeographed, 1968, pp. 9-10. Edited version of unpublished protocol.

6. *Ibid*, pp. 10-12. Edited version based on unpublished protocol of Carol S. Talbert.

7. Elizabeth Ann McPike, "Stigmatization: Its Facilitation and Func-

tion in an Elementary School," mimeographed, 1969, p. 6. Edited version of unpublished protocol.

8. Patricia Roberts, "Satisfaction of Dependency Needs and Conformity," p. 12. Edited version of unpublished protocol.

9. *Ibid.*, pp. 11-12. Edited version of unpublished protocol of Carol S. Talbert.

10. Carol S. Talbert, "The Weeding-Out Process: The Relation Between Black American English and Educational Achievement," mimeographed, 1972, pp. 31-32.

11. Patricia Roberts, "Satisfaction of Dependency Needs and Conformity," p. 13.

12. *Ibid.*

13. Ray C. Rist, *The Urban School: A Factory for Failure* (Cambridge: The MIT Press, 1973), p. 117.

14. Patricia Roberts, "Satisfaction of Dependency Needs and Conformity, " p. 14.

15. *Ibid.*, pp. 14-15.

16. *Ibid.*, p. 15.

17. *Ibid.*, p. 16.

18. *Ibid.*

19. Jules Henry, Second Quarterly Progress Report, p. 15. Describing this as "mitigated exclusion," Jules Henry commented on how being isolated in such a manner might affect the feelings of a child about himself and the teacher: "Here exclusion, as a mode of discipline and control, is infused with pleasure components: contact with the teacher and the book. This ambiguity might tend to cancel out the disciplinary component in exclusion."

20. Patricia Roberts, "Satisfaction of Dependency Needs and Conformity," p. 16.

21. *Ibid.*

22. *Ibid.*, p. 17. Edited version of unpublished protocol by Carol S. Talbert.

23. *Ibid.*, p. 18.

24. Desmond P. Ellis and Robert L. Hamblin, "Programmed Exchanges and the Control of Aggression" (prepared for the Bureau of Research, Office of Education, U.S. Department of Health, Education and Welfare, November 1966), p. 17.

25. Bruce Zelkovitz, "Disruptive Behavior in a Ghetto Kindergarten: An Exploratory Perspective," mimeographed, 1969; "Disruptive Behavior in Ghetto Schools, Part 1: A Reconceptualization," mimeographed, 1969. Unpublished protocols on observations in Mrs. McAllester's and Mrs. Pickett's classrooms.

CHAPTER
3 The Favored Few.

Well, many of these children will go on. Most will finish elementary school and most of them, I believe, will start in high school. Some will drop out, though. A few of them will finish high school and start college. I am trying to say that I don't think that the school is going to make that much difference. If it does, you won't really be able to say. I feel some will be successful, but most will be at the same level as their parents. Some will be on relief. Now I would say that when this generation grows up the percentage on relief (55% in the school currently) should decrease and that will be an accomplishment in itself.[1]

—Elementary school principal

This school principal's assessment of the potential of the students in his school echoed the judgment of the other staff members in the school system serving the black community. The members of the school board, the superintendent, other principals, the teachers, and the rest of the school personnel often voiced similar beliefs. There was a consensus among them about how few of the pupils in their charge would "make it" in school and in later life. Moreover, they were convinced that they had sound reasons for making these harsh judgments about most of the children in their classes. Since so few of the students in these elementary schools had ever finished high school, the principals and teachers assumed that the past would simply repeat itself. The hard facts were that very few of their pupils had been successful in school, while many had been failures.[2]

It was also taken for granted by the teachers and administrators that a large number of the students in the elementary schools in this district were "basically low achievers." Many were expected to do very poorly in their schoolwork, be held back, and eventually drop out of school at some point. The teachers agreed with the principal that the school and teaching were not "going to make that much difference" in how much the pupils learned. It was the home that would count most, and the school could do little to change its influence, either positive or negative, on a child's school experience. Most of the homes, according to the school staff, hurt rather than helped the children's chances to learn in school. Feeling they had made great efforts to teach as best they could, the teachers frequently recounted their personal experiences with children whom they had tried in vain to teach. This record of teacher frustration coupled with the poor performance of a majority of the students was used to justify the mood of defeat that pervaded the school system.

But this feeling of pessimism was not based solely on the teachers' individual frustrations, nor on actual records of failure of the pupils attending the schools. Rather it was a set of ideas and attitudes—an ideology—which was transmitted in explicit terms to the student teachers while they attended the city's teachers' college where virtually all of them were prepared for positions in the ghetto schools. The teachers-in-training were exposed to an ideology of failure before they had any classroom experience of their own. Such an outlook was also passed along by the principals to their staffs and by experienced teachers to new teachers before the latter had time to make up their own minds about the abilities of their pupils. The old buildings, the poor equipment, the large classes, and the run-down neighborhoods also lent support to the sense of discouragement. All this seemed to reinforce the staff's view that it was rational to devote more of the limited resources at hand to the most promising students. It would "make sense," as they often said, to concentrate on those children who were the most capable, especially since, in their opinion, slum life had made so many of the children not only very difficult to teach but also almost impossible to discipline. For these practical reasons, the teachers felt it would be foolish and wasteful to make much of an investment in the poor-risk children.

It was not surprising, then, that in all the classrooms observed during the three years of the research project the teachers established some formal or informal track system to divide the children into separate teaching groups. The groups were usually formed according to what the teacher explained were different levels of learning ability. Only one of the 11 classrooms studied in the four elementary schools was not divided in this way, but in this room all of the students had in a previous year been assigned to a "low" track, so they could still be regarded as tracked by means of segregation in a single classroom. The teachers referred to the children in these tracks as their "highs" and "lows," "stars" and "non-stars," giving them names such as the Tigers, Cardinals, and Clowns or table 1, table 2, and table 3.

There was considerable evidence for thinking that many of the teachers—even kindergarten teachers—judged the academic potential of their students very soon after school opened in the fall. In a classroom observed by Ray Rist, the teacher made permanent seating assignments for the children in her kindergarten on the eighth day of school.[3] At this time she placed each child at one of three tables, and the children remained at these tables for the rest of the year. Whatever basis she used for this early assignment to a high, middle, or low table, it did not include any kind of formal standardized testing, since no tests were administered until the spring of the kindergarten year when the pupils were given their first intelligence tests.

The use of ability groups for teaching the children was very inflexible. The composition of the groups remained the same throughout the day no matter what subject or activity was scheduled. This meant that the pupils were never shifted from one group to another on the basis of an individual child's being stronger in some areas and weaker in others. The children did not switch from their assigned group to another where they might profit from special instruction or from the stimulation of being on another reading level or in a different arithmetic grouping. Labeled and pigeonholed on the basis of what a teacher perceived as some kind of general capacity to follow the rules and do schoolwork, the pupils were treated as though their abilities were identical in all subject areas, as if they were "smart," "mediocre," or "dumb" in all aspects of the curriculum. Once put in a track, the student almost always stayed there permanently.

The research staff who were observers in the classrooms watched all of the kindergarten teachers sort out their pupils into ability groupings at some point in the fall. In the classroom in which the teacher assigned permanent seats to the youngsters at three tables after only eight days of school, the teacher had located the tables at different distances from the blackboard. She placed the "fast learners"—the most verbal and aggressive children—at table 1 which was closest to the front blackboard where she stood to conduct most of the lessons. Table 2 was set back farther from the teacher and the blackboard and table 3 was even more distant. The children assigned to table 2 and table 3 were considered less verbal and also less responsive by the teacher. Throughout the year she frequently completely ignored the pupils at these tables while concentrating her attention on the children seated closest to her at the first table. As the school year progressed, the children who were not sitting at table 1 became more and more disengaged from the lessons being taught at the front of the room. By late May these children had little communication with the teacher and almost no involvement in classroom activities.

When these kindergarten pupils entered the first grade the next fall, not one of the children seated at either table 2 or table 3 was assigned to the table of "fast learners." The marks and tests in kindergarten—the reading readiness scores—were very influential on the way the teacher organized the first-grade class. In fact, these records made it unnecessary for the first-grade teacher to judge the pupils on more intuitive grounds. She placed the children who had been at tables 2 and 3 at tables B and C in her room with no hesitation. Thus it turned out that the seating arrangement created by the kindergarten teacher from her own subjective assessment of the students' potential emerged in the first grade as a rigid assignment that was perpetuated the following year and kept any child from moving from the back of the room to the front. This was true even though the outcome of the intelligence tests given at the end of the

kindergarten year did not square in every case with the kindergarten teacher's evaluation of her pupils' "native abilities." It
turned out that not all of the children she had seated at table 1 had
higher I.Q. scores than the pupils she had assigned to the slower
groups.

In the following year when these first graders were joined by
pupils from other classes and some newcomers to make up a
second-grade class, they were once again divided into three ability
groupings which the teacher called Tigers, Cardinals, and Clowns.
The teacher assigned the pupils with the highest reading scores in
their first-grade material to the Tigers, those in the middle to the
Cardinals, and the lowest to the Clowns. Students who had been
seated at table A in the first grade were assigned to the Tigers, those
who had been at table B to the Cardinals, and the Clowns were
largely second-grade repeaters.

Keeping the original seating plan was virtually preordained by
the way the instructional materials were organized and taught according to ability groupings in the two preceding years. In the first
grade the three reading groups had been assigned different books to
read and no child in a lower group could forge ahead and catch up
with a higher reading group. Each student had to wait for the other
members of the group to finish a book before going on to the next
one. It was impossible for a child to demonstrate that he could
learn at a faster rate or master more difficult material. Each student was caught in a static definition of his abilities from which it
was virtually impossible to escape. Once categorized by a teacher as
a "slow learner," a student was kept to the pace of the reading
group to which the teacher thought he belonged. No matter how
well a child performed in that group or what potential he may have
had for keeping up with the children placed ahead of him, he could
not break out of the closed system. As might be expected, when
tested at the end of the year, the students earned marks which
generally reflected the different levels of instructional material to
which they had been exposed.

The teacher of this second-grade room distributed rewards to all
of the children rather sparingly, even to the Tigers. However, she
gave the Tigers a good deal more praise and support than the
Clowns. When the observer coded the teacher's interaction with the

second graders, he found that she used between two and five times as much control-oriented behavior—as distinct from supportive or neutral behavior—with the Clowns as with the Tigers. She explained to the observer that the Clowns were "slow and disinterested." But assuming that neutral and supportive behavior on the part of the teacher would have been more encouraging than punishment and other control-oriented behavior, it was likely that the Clowns could have benefited from the positive learning situation which some praise and extra help from the teacher might have created. The further fact that the Clowns were the most physically isolated from the teacher and received the least amount of her teaching time suggested that there might have been good reason for the Clowns' being "slow and disinterested."

In almost all the classrooms observed, the teachers tended to interact both more frequently and more favorably with those "doing well" than with those "doing poorly." In fact, the teachers tended to make the lessons revolve around a very few students, concentrating largely on those who could give the correct answers. Of course, it cannot be assumed that the amount of interaction with the teacher would necessarily be synonymous with learning. Indeed, it could be argued that teacher-dominated classrooms—even those with positive overtones—might result in less learning. Being ignored by the teacher might actually allow a child to develop and experiment on his own. But the children in these classrooms were not permitted either freedom to move around the room or freedom to learn independently. As in other public schools in the ghetto, most of the children were glued to their seats and to the teacher's daily schedule. They were not allowed to engage in creative activities or to exercise any urge to learn that they might have felt. Bureaucratic needs overrode everything else. Quiet, neatness, and order were the rule. It was not just that the children were ignored but that they were forced to sit in their seats with no alternative kinds of activities tolerated—activities that might have been conducive to learning. The usual routine followed in Mrs. Bobb's room was described by Carol Talbert in some detail:

In Mrs. Bobb's first-grade class, the first few time segments in the morning are taken up with the inevitable collection of lunch money, the "Pledge of

Allegiance to the Flag," and the "Song of the Flag." School then begins in earnest with the teacher asking one of the "preferred" students to read the weather calendar. A discussion of the weather follows, the teacher asking each child in turn to describe the weather until she gets the right answer. The teacher then writes the appropriate weather conditions on the board, for example, "Today is cloudy." The children are then told to copy this sentence from the blackboard.

At this point the differences in the performance of pupils are evident. Some quickly and deftly draw letters and headings on their papers while others begin to launch into repetitive erasing and rewriting. In the back of the room some draw a few random letters on their papers, but the rear-of-the-room children spend a lot of time gazing into space, resting their heads on their books, and chatting with each other. Periodically, they fall from their chairs with a great clatter. Usually if one child falls another will follow quickly. Meanwhile the teacher praises the work of the good students and berates the others for their poor performance. The teacher herself is aware of the onus of being in the back of the room and frequently warns a child that if he doesn't shape up she will remove him from the front and put him in the back.

Following this introductory lesson the teacher allocates the lesson time between the various reading groups. She usually gathers the "high readers" around her, telling the remaining students to continue copying from the blackboard. While her high group reads with her, the remaining children write and erase. They gradually lose interest and begin to draw and color pictures or play with each other. Following this period the children of the advanced reading group "help" the others. The helpers guide the other children's hands, advise them, and remind them of all the mistakes they are making.

The lessons during the remainder of the day follow much the same routine, with the few children who are most involved with the teacher answering most of her questions. The children in this group sit directly in front of the teacher and to the side on the first few seats. This is especially crucial to teacher-student interaction since the teacher rarely leaves her desk. Only children in the high group approach her desk and feel confident enough to begin rummaging through it. Patricia, one of the "best" students, moves around the room very freely, touching the teacher as she passes by her desk.

The pattern of hand raising in response to the teacher's questions is notice-
ably different for the high and low groups—the favored children almost
leap out of their seats to answer a question whereas the others raise their
hands cautiously.

The teacher has a tendency to rely first on her high group and later move to
the others for answers and recitals, eventually involving most of the
children in her lessons and the question-and-answer sessions. But as the day
wears on, many of the children spend the time in inactivity—doing
nothing; they alternate between whispering, passing things, occasionally
engaging in physical contact play, and just sitting.[4]

When Carol Talbert made observations in two black kindergartens and recorded the interaction between the teachers and
pupils at separate intervals (September, then January, and again in
April), she found that the frequency of interaction between the
teachers and children decreased markedly between September and
April.[5] Characteristic of these fewer interactions was a change in
the proportion of positive and negative responses by the teachers to
the children. As the year progressed the teachers spent relatively
less time giving positive responses and more time responding to the
children negatively. There was also an increasing number of
children who received no response at all from the teachers. In fact,
by April there were only a few pupils with whom the teachers interacted at all most of the time. These few children were primarily
girls who belonged to the "high" reading group. They had become
the recipients of the teachers' many favorable gestures, touches,
smiles, positive comments, and special privileges granted to their
chosen helpers. These pupils handed out material to the class and
ran errands around the school, carrying messages to the office and
to other teachers. They spent more time with the teachers than the
other students either in oral recitation or in getting and holding the
teachers' attention for some other purpose, and they were likely to
sustain this relationship throughout the school year.

Complaining repeatedly that they were prevented by lack of time
from giving all of the children the attention they needed, the
teachers concentrated their energies mainly on teaching a limited
number of students while permitting the remainder of the children

to just "put in their time." When organizing their classes in the fall, the kindergarten teachers observed by Talbert gave a good deal of attention, albeit of a negative sort, to the children who did not readily join in the classroom activities, the extremely shy and withdrawn ones. However, they directed the lion's share of their negative responses toward the boys rather than the girls. In one class, the boys received about five and a half times as many negative reactions from the teacher as the girls, and in the other room, almost three times as many. After these initial efforts to bring all the children into the group as participants failed to work, the teachers allowed those children who failed to respond to their gestures to remove themselves to the edges of the group. The teachers then spent less time criticizing and punishing them. In fact, the teacher in one of the kindergartens never treated one-third of the children in her room in anything but an impersonal way while the other teacher treated about one-fifth of her kindergartners in this way.

The children in this group in turn appeared to respond to the teacher's being less negative by settling down and adjusting to the way they were treated. The decrease in the negative responses by the teachers toward this group of children resulted in the crystallization of a peripheral group later in the school year. The separate activities of this group increased as the school year proceeded. The "low" students tended to tune out of classroom activities a good deal of the time. When they were not looking out the window or talking among themselves in almost imperceptible whispers, they were writing, drawing, and erasing, and then writing, drawing, and erasing again. One thing they seemed to be learning was to be painstakingly neat in their work. These children on the periphery, especially the boys, were also learning to tolerate extreme boredom.

Another research team member, Marco Pardi, studied the specific differences in the behavior of teachers toward high achievers and low achievers and attempted to measure the effects of the frequency of positive and negative interactions with the teachers on the self-esteem of the children.[6] Four classrooms—a first grade, a fourth grade, a fifth grade, and a sixth grade—were selected for study. For each class, two students selected by their teachers as a high achiever and a low achiever were monitored for five hours as they interacted with their teacher. It turned out that the high achievers engaged in more positive interaction with their teachers and the low achievers in more negative interactions. Later when the children were interviewed individually it was found that their feelings of high self-esteem were associated with being classified by the teacher as high achievers and their feelings of low self-esteem with being identified as low achievers.

The "low" students in the classrooms we observed not only suffered feelings of low esteem about themselves and isolation from the teacher, but also were the butt of ridicule and belittlement by students in the high group. As the children in the high groups began to internalize the positive attitudes of the teacher toward themselves, they also absorbed the negative attitudes of the teacher toward many of the other children in the class. They were allowed and even encouraged to lord it over children in the low groups, while being spared the humiliating experience of being bossed around and scorned by children their own age. Members of the high group frequently took on the role of teacher in maintaining order in the classroom and urging conformity to the teacher's rules when she was out of the room. Downgrading remarks frequently flowed from children in the high group toward those in the low but rarely from the low to the high:

David came to where I was seated and told me to look at the shoes that Lilly was wearing to school. I asked him why I should look at the shoes and he responded, "Cause they so ragged and dirty." (David sits at table 1 and Lilly at table 3.)

Susan has brought two magazines from home. She is at her table looking through one of them. Mrs. Caplow comes to Susan and asks if she would like to share the magazine she is not reading with another child. Before Susan can reply, Frank comes and takes a magazine from Susan, commenting, "She don't need a magazine." (Frank is from table 1, Susan from table 3.)[7]

One frequent response of children in the low groups to their plight was to develop tightly knit friendship groups. In several classrooms, this was more common among boys than girls. The girls tended to be more oriented to the teacher or were loners, while boys looked to each other for companionship and support.

But these friendship bonds among some of the boys in the low group had a somewhat fragile quality. In one second-grade classroom, the group that had the strongest friendship bonds also rejected members of their own group on certain occasions. In one kindergarten, the children in the lower groups were frequently seen mirroring toward each other the attitudes of the teacher and the "high" students toward them. "Low" students called each other "stupid," "dummy," and "dumb-dumb." They taunted each other with threats of beatings, "whoppins," and spitting. This, of course, did not necessarily mean that there was less solidarity or affection among them. Several other types of responses were made by these children to the situation they faced in the classroom: some withdrew and made few responses, some began to copy and mimic each other, others instigated disruption, and still others attempted to hoard a large number of toys and supplies.

There was one room which was an exception to the others in that it did not have the harsh atmosphere that generally pervaded the classrooms in the black schools. This was a first-grade class composed of children with average and below-average rankings and whose teacher, Mrs. Webb, was more democratic in her methods than the others. Researcher Mark Schoepfle made a study of the visible effects of Mrs. Webb's teaching techniques upon the behavior of the children in her classroom.[8] He compared her teaching with that of Mrs. Bobb who was more authoritarian in the way she conducted her advanced first grade composed of pupils who were beginning to read. Using a 9-point plus-and-minus coding scheme, Schoepfle found that Mrs. Bobb rewarded her favored four children much more frequently than the rest of the pupils. The "faster" students in her room were allowed to wander about the room, speak out without the teacher's permission, and "help" the "slower" children.

Mrs. Webb, on the other hand, actively sought to avoid favoritism by using various democratic techniques. She rarely neglected to reward a correct response made by any of her students. Although she divided the children into three different reading groups according to rate of progress, she did not create a hierarchy of dominance of an elite few over the others. In fact, there appeared to be no preferred group in her room. Notable was the absence of the commonly instituted teacher's helper, and no group of children seemed to emerge as peripheral to classroom activities.

In comparing how the pupils fared in these contrasting climates, Schoepfle found that the low achiever had a greater opportunity for self-assertion, social interaction, and imaginative behavior in the more democratic classroom. By contrast, in the authoritarian classroom there appeared to be a greater polarity of success and failure. In an authoritarian atmosphere, the child had to learn to stand or fall independently, a process which tended to accelerate his travel toward either pole, success or failure.

With the exception of Mrs. Webb's class, the schoolrooms were harsh places for these inner-city children to start an educational career. But the students were required by law to be there and they responded to the treatment by their teachers in various ways. According to Patricia Roberts, one of the research team members, the youngsters who were defined by their teachers as doing poorly and who had infrequent interaction with the teacher tended to give their full attention to classroom activities only when they were being directly supervised in their assignments but not when they were left on their own.[9] Comparing two children doing poorly with two others doing well in one kindergarten, Roberts found that all four of the children followed the teacher's instructions and obeyed her in essentially the same manner as long as she was watching them. However, during unsupervised play periods when she gave them games to play such as puzzles, pegs and boards, or building blocks, the difference in their participation was striking. For example, Henry and James, who were doing poorly, responded to the direct supervision of the teacher 16 out of 19 times and 15 out of 18 times, respectively, but when unsupervised Henry carried out the teacher's instructions only three out of 24 times and James only once in 20 situations. By contrast, Diane, who was doing well, responded positively to the teacher's supervision 13 out of 14 times, and in unsupervised play in 12 out of 14 situations. Like Diane, Ronald did not become inattentive when the teacher was not in charge of an activity. Ronald responded positively when the teacher was supervising 10 out of 11 times and, when left in an unsupervised play situation, 20 out of 22 times.

The children who were not doing well seemed to be demonstrating by their behavior that they needed more rather than less of their teacher's attention. At least they needed time, attention, and affection equal to that given the preferred pupils if they were to learn such curriculum skills as shape and color discrimination, hand-eye coordination, and judgment about depth and breadth which activities such as putting puzzles together, placing pegs in holes, and stacking blocks in a tower were intended to develop. As soon as Henry and James, for example, were allowed to be inattentive to these tasks during the so-called play periods, they were neglecting to lay the essential groundwork for the reading, writing, and arithmetic lessons in the offing. From the very beginning the children were being taught differently and were learning different amounts. They clearly had different needs that were going unattended. The question was, what in fact were they learning? Carol Talbert was of the opinion that at least three kinds of learning were occurring in the classrooms she observed:

In the central group are the active learners who, by virtue of their high interaction with the teacher, are able to benefit from instant feedback, immediate reinforcement and high repetition of teacher's instructions and directions. Passive members of this central group are also exposed to the lessons presented by the teacher and the behaviors of the ''star'' performers; these can be labeled vicarious learners. The third group . . . are no doubt learning a great deal, but it is not the kind of learning desired by the teacher . . . .

The peripheral learner is not in direct contact with the reading and arithmetic lessons or other necessary teaching experiences essential to later scholastic achievement. Since the general structure of elementary school instruction is based upon a sequential model in which lower levels must be mastered before progression to the next step, these peripheral pupils will almost certainly be severely handicapped when they are expected to meet the requirements of the first and later grades.[10]

On the question of whether the pupils on the edge of things learned anything in class, Ray Rist (who had been the observer in the kindergarten where intraclass tracking of the students was especially marked in their early and rigid assignment to tables 1, 2, and 3) thought the pupils at tables 2 and 3 learned much more than

their teacher realized. Although those seated at tables 2 and 3 were
systematically ignored by the teacher and participated in the lessons
much less than the pupils at table 1, they nevertheless did learn
some classroom material:

I contend that in fact they did learn, but in a fundamentally different way
from the way in which the high status children at Table 1 learned. The
children at Tables 2 and 3 who were unable to interact with the teacher
began to develop patterns of interaction among themselves whereby they
would discuss the material that the teacher was presenting to the children at
Table 1. Thus I have termed their method of grasping the material "secondary learning" to imply that knowledge was not gained in direct interaction
with the teacher, but through the mediation of peers and also through
listening to the teacher though she was not speaking to them.

That the children were grasping, in part, the material presented to the
classroom was apparent to me in home visits when the children who sat at
Table 3 would relate material specifically taught by the teacher to the
children at Table 1. It is not as though the children at Tables 2 and 3 were
ignorant of what was being taught in the class, but rather that the patterns
of classroom interaction established by the teacher inhibited the low status
children from verbalizing what knowledge they had accumulated. Thus,
from the teacher's frame of reference, those who could not discuss must
not know. Her expectations continued to be fulfilled, for though the low
status children had accumulated knowledge, they did not have the opportunity to verbalize it and, consequently, the teacher could not know what
they had learned. Children at Tables 2 and 3 had learned material presented
in the kindergarten classroom, but would continue to be defined by the
teacher as children who could not or would not learn.[11]

It was not possible to find out how much of this kind of secondary learning of classroom material was taking place, since the
children did not have the opportunity to demonstrate to their
teacher that they knew things which they were not being taught
directly. Maybe this secondary or vicarious way of learning seemed
natural to the children inasmuch as it bore some resemblence to the
way children in lower-class families are known to relate to adult
conversations. They are expected to listen without participating.
However, no member of the research team thought that secondary
learning in the classroom enabled the children to master their

school subjects sufficiently to compensate for the lack of direct instruction by their teachers. Talbert agreed that the children on the periphery were learning a great deal, but she did not think it was skills in reading, writing, and arithmetic needed for making adequate progress in these areas. Rist was mainly impressed by the extent to which the children expressed a desire to learn and by what they had picked up in class on their own.

Once a child was defined by the teacher as doing poorly, however, there was no chance that he could somehow make it on his own. He was slated to receive less instruction, attention, and affection from the teacher, participate less in class activities, and eventually withdraw to the sidelines. Good-natured or sullen, passive or hostile, compliant or troublesome, he did worse and worse in his schoolwork and, as the year progressed, he failed more and more often to live up to the academic standards of his grade level. Some children, it was true, had fun with each other in the back of the room when they gathered there for group activities. But for most, self-doubt and low self-esteem combined to create a fear of putting forth the increasingly difficult effort to catch up.

At this point the teachers interpreted a child's poor performance as a confirmation of their initial evaluation of his poor potential: "Well, he's just bound to fail. He's withdrawn and has emotional problems," or "He's just not verbal." His teachers rarely made any effort to teach him; as a consequence he did not learn because he was not taught. His poor record and teacher gossip preceded him into the next year's class and the one following that. The labels persisted in part because they became more and more real. The child believed them, and the teachers believed them. Failure for many had become a certainty. A kindergarten teacher's quick judgment had become a self-fulfilling prophecy.

The social structure of the classrooms observed tended to take on a castelike character, meaning that there was rarely any movement of students between the tracks or castes created by the teachers.[12] In addition, the teachers acted as if those in the low groups should be kept separate from those in the higher groups. It was as if the children assigned to the low groups could contaminate the potentially successful. Although the boundaries between the tracks were not impermeable, still a pupil rarely moved up from the bottom to the top where he would have access to more of the teacher's attention.

As the years went by and the children in the bottom tracks were promoted to the higher grades in the elementary schools, they became increasingly less responsive to school and participated only marginally in the school scene even when they were in attendance. One of the observers recorded a conversation with such children in fifth grade who were attending a school supposedly providing compensatory education and enrichment programs. These youngsters were already well along the path to becoming outsiders and they understood what was happening to their education:

As the researcher approached the door leading into the school building, he noticed that four young girls were seated on a railing just outside the door to the branch of School 1. Although he could not hear what they were saying, he could tell that they were talking about him. As they gazed toward him they lowered their voices, giggled and then said, "Hi! Who you is?"

Before the researcher could answer the girls made guesses at who the researcher was. One girl said, "You a substitute" and another guessed that the researcher was a teacher. The researcher replied that he was studying boys and girls and how they learn and was going into Mrs. Pickett's class to sit with the boys and girls. One of the girls said, "Oh" and the others stopped their questions about the identity of the researcher.

The researcher then said to them, "I see you're not in class now" and one of the girls explained the situation which had brought them outside. She said that she and the other girls had told Mrs. Tom, their fifth grade teacher, that they were wanted by Mr. West in the office to do some work there and she let them go without any questions or any note to the principal. All of the kids could get out of Mrs. Tom's class whenever they wanted to. "We just say we goin' to the office. All we have to do is say that Mr. West want us or anyone else."

The researcher then asked them what they do if they're not needed in the office. "Oh, we just sit outside." One of the girls who was very nattily attired in an immaculate plaid dress and a blue sweater said, "We don't have no books." The researcher said, "No books in the class?" and all of the girls nodded. One of them then described their usual class procedure: apparently Mrs. Tom does not use textbooks in the fifth grade class or at least has not as yet. She tells the boys and girls to bring their own pencils and pieces of paper to the classroom. When they take their seats at the beginning of the day, she either tells them to draw pictures or write a story. If a student does not have his or her own pencil or piece of paper, Mrs. Tom will not furnish any of these items for them. They just sit there quietly and do nothing for the remainder of the day.

One of the girls observed, "By the time we get to sixth grade, boy, we be dumb." One of the other girls said, "We do nothing, we do nothing." And then the girl in the plaid described how Mrs. Tom walks around the class and if a boy or girl is making a noise, she pinches them on the arm. Giving a demonstration to the researcher she said, "She have sharp nails."[13]

In these schools where the ideology of failure was so firmly entrenched, the staffs opted for concentrating on those children whom they believed were destined for success. The teachers were expected to give the majority of their limited time and energy to a select few and neglect the education of most of the others. Paying attention to the few with "payoff" helped establish the feeling that they were accomplishing something if they had put a few students through the system. It also created a more rewarding environment for the teachers. Their self-esteem, if nothing else, demanded some success with some students.

There is a folklore of democracy in the American school system. Its core tenet is that education is the great equalizer. A high school diploma is the gateway to the "great American dream." But the corollary is that the good life comes only to those who work hard and compete successfully. This myth gives the teacher the means to excuse her failure as a teacher when she is not able to "equalize" the distance between the children in her classroom. After all, if Jimmy doesn't want to work, how can she help him be a success?

Notes

1. Ray C. Rist, *The Urban School: A Factory for Failure* (Cambridge: The MIT Press, 1973), p. 49.

2. During the 1968-69 school year, the dropout rate from poverty-area high schools was 25.6 percent compared with 11.9 percent in nonpoverty-

area high schools. In 1970, more than 900 of the 2,100 elementary class-rooms in the poverty area had 36 or more pupils and more than 400 substitute teachers in regular classroom assignments.

3. See Rist, *The Urban School*, and "Student Social Class and Teacher Expectations: The Self-Fulfilling Prophecy in Ghetto Education," *Harvard Educational Review* 40 (1970) for his detailed account of observations made in one of the classes over a three-year period.

4. Carol S. Talbert, "The Weeding-Out Process: The Relation Between Black American English and Educational Achievement," mimeographed, 1972, pp. 32-33.

5. See Carol S. Talbert, "Interaction and Adaptation in Two Negro Kindergartens," *Human Organization* 29 (Summer 1970), pp. 103-114.

6. Marco Pardi, "A Pilot Study of Classroom Attitudinal Differentials and Their Meanings to the Students" (master's thesis, 1969).

7. Rist, *The Urban School*, pp. 115-16.

8. Mark Schoepfle, "A Pilot Study of the Ecology of Classroom Behavior," mimeographed, 1969, pp. 7-26.

9. Patricia Roberts, "Satisfaction of Dependency Needs and Conformity," mimeographed, 1969, pp. 1-22.

10. Talbert, "Interaction and Adaptation in Two Negro Kindergartens," p. 113.

11. Ray C. Rist, "The Socialization of the Ghetto Child into the Urban School System" (Ph.D. dissertation, 1970), pp. 382-83.

12. Ibid.

13. Bruce Zelkovitz, "Disruptive Behavior in Ghetto Schools, Part 1: A Reconceptualization," mimeographed, 1969, pp. 9-10.

CHAPTER 4
The Weeding-Out Process

*Well, every one of these kids is going to go out some
day and get some sort of job. There are so many
jobs, there's always a job for somebody, so every kid
will find his place. Somebody will be a garbage
collector, another will be a dock worker, another one
will be a doctor or lawyer. It doesn't really make any
difference which one. The rule we always go by here
is—whatever you are, be the best. And fortunately,
for a lot of these kids who just can't seem to get
ahead, we have special classes now so that they can
get more special attention.*[1]

　　　　　　—Kindergarten teacher in a ghetto school

A teacher expressed these views when she was asked to reflect on
the future of the children in her kindergarten class. Like the other
teachers in the inner-city schools under observation, she appeared
to have no doubt about her ability to size up her pupils' chances for
success or failure in school without the benefit of objective testing
of their abilities. Her judgments about the potential of each child
were made early in the school year and they did not seem to be particularly difficult for her to make. Efficiency demanded little vacil-
lation, and she quickly chose which child she expected would be the
garbage collector, dock worker, doctor, or lawyer. She selected
those pupils who were the most promising and separated them from
those who were not. The culling was done with a sure hand since
she felt very confident about her decisions. She would not be asked
to justify the assignment of her pupils to one category or another.

Nor did she have to worry about anyone calling her to task for her selections. Indeed, everyone in the school would agree with how she evaluated the children's potential. The principal and the other teachers would go along with her judgments—they had always agreed with each other's evaluations in the past.

So, as school opened in the fall, the teachers controlled the fates of their young pupils as they went about the business of deciding where to place each child in the stratified order of their classrooms, an order which paralleled their ideas of the world outside. They thought of themselves as realists. However, they were not necessarily conscious of the criteria they used in making these judgments about their new students. Interviews with teachers probing for information about how they evaluated the pupils were relatively unproductive. Typical were the responses of a teacher who said she believed that some students were "just basically low achievers" and others were "high achievers." Some of the children were "fast learners" and others had "no idea what was going on in the classroom." Whatever the criteria used to evaluate the students' potential, the judgments could only be described as intuitive, since they were not based on objective data.

However, the teachers did have access to various kinds of background information about the children before making up their minds about how they would rank them. Available to the teachers in one school, for example, were a number of facts about the family of each child as well as other information that the school collected for its files. It included the composition of a child's family, including whether he lived with both, one, or neither of his natural parents and the number of children in the family. The school registration forms contained the names and addresses of a child's parents or guardians, their occupations, and telephone number, if they had one. The registration forms also listed the preschool experience of the child, the name of the family doctor, if there was one, and health information listing the child's immunizations and any special physical conditions. The parents were asked to complete a behavioral questionnaire about the entering pupil which included a checklist of whether he had special problems, such as thumbsucking, bedwetting, lying, and stealing. In addition, the school maintained a list of the families on welfare. If a child came from a welfare home, ADC (standing for Aid to Dependent Children) was printed by hand in red at the top of his permanent transcript. In addition to their knowledge based on this written information, the teachers were often already acquainted with a child's family by reputation or from previous teaching contacts with his older siblings. The teachers also frequently learned about their new pupils and their families from other teachers. Those families who already had a reputation among the teaching staff were categorized roughly into three groups: "good people," "never see them," and "troublemakers."

Whatever method the teachers used to assign their pupils to ability groups, there were observable differences in the characteristics of the children who were placed in the higher and lower groups. For example, in the kindergarten in which the teacher made permanent seating assignments to one of three tables on the eighth day of school, a child's appearance was a sure clue to where he would be seated.[2] The children at table 1 were dressed better than the others. Their clothes were relatively new, of good quality, and kept clean and well pressed. On the other hand, most of the children at table 2 and, with only one exception, all of the children at table 3 were shabbily dressed in old clothes that were often quite dirty. In the winter months, the difference in the quality and warmth of the children's clothes was even more noticeable. The "high" children sitting at the table closest to the teacher wore heavy coats and sweaters in cold weather, but those at the other two tables were often still wearing their spring coats, summer dresses, or thin cotton slacks even on severely cold days. The only child in the lowest stream who was appropriately dressed for the change of seasons came from a home in which the mother was on welfare but received clothing from her brother and sister for her children to wear.

Another difference in the physical appearance of the children assigned to the three tables was their skin color and the condition of their hair. Although the students were not seated at the different tables according to skin color in every case, there were more children at the third table with very dark skin (five out of ten, or one-half) than there were at the first table (three out of nine, or one-third). All of the children at the first table came to school with well-groomed hair. The three boys at this table all had short haircuts, and the six girls at the same table had their hair processed and neatly combed. Two boys and three girls out of the ten children at the second table had either matted or unprocessed hair; the number of children with matted or unprocessed hair increased to eight (four boys and four girls out of 11, or more than three-fourths) at the third table.

Another distinction was the presence or absence of body odor. While none of the top children came to school with the odor of urine, there were two children in the middle group and five children in the lowest one who frequently smelled of urine. The teacher was very sensitive to how the children smelled and asked the researcher if he would speak to the mothers of some of the "low" children about bathing and changing their underwear.

The children in the various tracks also interacted with each other and the teacher differently. Several of the children tried to take charge of the class from the outset, giving orders to other children, choosing up sides for games on the playground, and speaking on behalf of the entire class to the teacher ("We want to color now"). These children were all placed by the teacher at table 1. This same group of children was generally at ease in their interaction with the teacher, often crowding around her closely. The children assigned to table 2 and table 3, on the other hand, rarely came near the teacher; they usually stayed at the outer edges of the group that clustered around her.

The children in this kindergarten also differed in the amount they talked, to whom they talked, and the language they used. The children placed at the first table were quite verbal. They were quick to answer the teacher's questions, and they talked a good deal in an informal way with the teacher and the other children, particularly with their friends at the same table. The children placed at the other two tables spoke much less often with the teacher and answered questions she put to them directly much less frequently. The "no response" rate to teacher questions was nearly three to one for the children seated at tables 2 and 3 in comparison with table 1. In addition, the children placed at the first table were more likely to use Standard English in the classroom. As in most of the classrooms observed, this kindergarten teacher used both Standard English and Black English at various times when speaking to the class, but the children seated at the last two tables often responded to the teacher in Black English while the children at the first table did so infrequently. In other words, the children at the first table were much more familiar with "school language" and used it more often. When the teacher spoke Standard English, the top students responded in kind.

When the students' records were examined, it was found that the children assigned by the teacher to the first table and those seated at the others came from families of differing socioeconomic status. Although it is not known to what extent the teacher made use of the information available to her about the children's family backgrounds when she assigned them to tracks, this teacher made a seating plan which did in fact reflect the social status differences between the children. Table I compares some of the social and economic characteristics of the children's families according to where the students had been placed by the teacher. As shown by the table, the distribution of the children coincided very closely with their families' income, education, composition, and size. For instance, none of the families of children seated at table 1 were on welfare or had a total family income below $3,000 a year, while two of the children at table 2 and four of the children at table 1 were from families on welfare; likewise, four of the children at table 2 and seven of the children at table 3 came from families with incomes below $3,000 a year. While four of the children at table 1 were from families with incomes above $12,000, none of the children at the other two tables had families in this high an income bracket. Parents of the children at table 1 had more education. In addition, six of the nine at table 1 had both parents present in the home, while only three out of 11 at table 2 and two out of 10 at table 3 had both parents present. The average number of siblings was between three and four at table 1, between five and six at table 2, and between six and seven at table 3.

Thus, the "faster learners" came from families of a higher socioeconomic level than the children placed at lower tables. These children also happened to wear better clothes, look neat, and smell good. Their parents were apt to be better educated, steadily employed, and living together. With fewer children in their families,

Table I

**Distribution of Socioeconomic Status Factors by
Seating Arrangement at the Three Tables
in the Kindergarten Classroom**

	Seating Arrangement*		
Factors	*Table 1*	*Table 2*	*Table 3*
INCOME			
Families on welfare	0	2	4
Families with father employed	6	3	2
Families with mother employed	5	5	5
Families with both parents employed	5	3	2
Total family income below $3,000/yr.**	0	4	7
Total family income above $12,000/yr.**	4	0	0
EDUCATION			
Father ever grade school	6	3	2
Father ever high school	5	2	1
Father ever college	1	0	0
Mother ever grade school	9	10	8
Mother ever high school	7	6	5
Mother ever college	4	0	0
Children with preschool experience	1	1	0

Table I (cont.)

FAMILY SIZE

Families with one child	3	1	0
Families with six or more children	2	6	7
Average number of siblings in family	3-4	5-6	6-7
Families with both parents present	6	3	2

*There are 9 children at table 1, 11 children at table 2, and 10 children at table 3.
**Estimated from stated occupation

Source: Ray C. Rist, "Student Social Class and Teacher Expectations: The Self-Fulfilling Prophecy in Ghetto Education," *Harvard Educational Review* 40 (August 1970), p. 421. Copyright© 1970 by President and Fellows of Harvard College.

the students at table 1 came from families who had more time and material resources to spend on them. All this gave promise of a child who, according to the teacher, would be willing and eager to learn and whose parents would take an interest in their child's progress in school and expect the child to work hard and perform well. The children whose families possessed the fewest of all of these qualities had the poorest outlook and the ones who fell between the two extremes were not as badly off as the bottom group but they had a greater chance of becoming failures than successes.

The "high" children, who tended to be more verbal both in the frequency of their response to questions and in their interaction with other children, also appeared to be more adept at code-switching between Black English and Standard English in appropriate situations. Quite often the teacher used Black English under circumstances when she was being emotionally supportive or talking individually to the children but she used Standard English for most of her formal teaching. When exposed to the code-switching of their teachers, it is possible that the high achievers could go along with their speech pattern so easily because they heard their parents change from Black English to Standard English at home.

There appeared to be a sexual difference, too, in that girls code-switched more easily than boys.

When the children finished kindergarten and went on to the first grade the following year, their teachers retained virtually the same groupings that had been created by kindergarten teachers. The following year in the second grade, many of the children who had been together in kindergarten were no longer a part of the group. Those who had made unsatisfactory progress had been held back, and many others had moved out of the school district. At this juncture there were a number of school records available to the teacher for making up ability groupings, among which were pupils' grades in kindergarten and first grade, reading scores on a series of diagnostic tests given at the end of first grade, teacher evaluations, and IQ scores. When asked how she decided to divide up the children, the teacher said that the single most important factor determining the seating arrangement was the first-grade reading scores. However, she explained that she had placed two children in the middle group who had been in the highest group in first grade because she had to have someone in that group who would be able to give the correct answer. She said that she did not want to waste time teaching the middle group if there was no one in it to respond. She also placed a child in the lowest group who had formerly been in a middle group for the same reason, since she felt that teaching the Clowns would be "mostly a waste of time" and she wanted "at least one student in the bunch who would give a correct answer." Thus some of the pupils were assigned seats on the basis of the teacher's need rather than according to their reading scores.

According to Table II, the teacher's placement of the children in the Tigers, Cardinals, and Clown also coincided very closely with their families' income, amount of education, composition, and size. The distribution of socioeconomic status factors according to ability groups, therefore, remained essentially unchanged from the kindergarten year.

In another kindergarten where there were no children at all from middle-income families, there were still some differences in the family status of the children who were in the high and low reading groups. Table III shows that the children in the high reading group were likely to come from homes in slightly better economic circum-

Table II

**Distribution of Socioeconomic Status Factors by
Seating Arrangement in the Three Reading Groups
in the Second-Grade Classroom**

	Reading Group		
Factors	*Tigers*	*Cardinals*	*Clowns*
INCOME			
Families on welfare	2	4	7
Families with father employed	8	5	1
Families with mother employed	7	11	6
Families with both parents employed	7	5	1
Total family income below $3,000/yr.**	1	5	8
Total family income above $12,000/yr.**	4	0	0

EDUCATION

Father ever grade school	8	6	1
Father ever high school	7	4	0
Father ever college	0	0	0
Mother ever grade school	12	13	9
Mother ever high school	9	7	4
Mother ever college	3	0	0
Children with preschool experience	1	0	0

Table II (cont.)

FAMILY SIZE

Families with one child	2	0	1
Families with six or more children	3	8	5
Average number of siblings in family	3-4	6-7	7-8
Families with both parents present	8	6	1

*There are 12 children in the Tiger group, 14 children in the Cardinal group, and 9 children in the Clown group.

**Estimated from stated occupation

Source: Ray C. Rist, "Student Social Class and Teacher Expectations: The Self-Fulfilling Prophecy in Ghetto Education," *Harvard Educational Review* 40 (August 1970), p. 434. Copyright© 1970 by President and Fellows of Harvard College.

stances. In this room, there were more girls in the high reading group than boys. Of the 14 children in the high reading group, 11 were girls; of the 17 children in the low reading group, only five were girls.

In an attempt to understand the sources of teacher preference for certain children, Carol Talbert made a study of a first-grade class which she had observed previously during their kindergarten year. The kindergarten teacher had created a situation which allowed her to concentrate on a few favored pupils—her pets—while the rest of the children existed in a kind of twilight zone. Among these latter children there were two divisions: a small cohesive group, the "troublemakers," who spent time together at the back of the room talking surreptitiously and entertaining each other; and a second, larger group who were not members of the active periphery and who never received any verbal response at all from the teacher once the classroom was organized. Members of this larger group who were neither pets nor troublemakers were cast in the role of "phantom" children. After the first few months of kindergarten, the children in the class separated quickly into the three groups and no child who was a troublemaker or a phantom ever became a high achiever and none of the pets ever fell from grace into one of the unfavored groups.

What combination of factors influenced the teacher favorably or unfavorably toward the children in this classroom? The following year when they entered first grade, Talbert made a particular effort to focus attention on this question. In the early months of the school year when the class was being introduced to their first reading experiences, a few central or star children had already emerged. Talbert, therefore, assumed that there were certain characteristics—possibly their behavior, attitudes, appearance, or background—to which the teacher was reacting as a basis for her preferences. As a way of examining what student traits were affecting the teacher's judgment, the researcher gave the teacher slips of paper on which the children's names were written and asked her to rank them in ascending order from the "prospective least successful" to the "prospective most successful." The results of this ranking were then compared with the child's sex, family structure, friendship choices, and reading level.

After the 28 pupils who had been ranked by their teacher were divided at midpoint into the highs and the lows, the sex of the child was compared with the teacher's ranking. Did being a girl have a bearing on a child's position? Talbert was interested in determining this since so many of the teachers' pets were girls. As indicated in Table IV, of the 28 pupils, eight of those placed in the top half of the class by the teacher were girls and five in the bottom half were girls, while there were six boys in the high group and nine in the low. Although this appeared to show some degree of teacher preference for girls, Gerry and James, two of the boys who were in the top group, were repeatedly the objects of favorable treatment by the teacher. Conversely, some of the girls received very little of the teacher's attention.

While the dichotomous classification *girl* or *boy* seemed to have had some bearing on the teacher's ranking, it did not answer the question, Does the teacher prefer boys who act girlish and girls who act least boyish? Classroom observations seemed to indicate a

Table III

**Socioeconomic Differences of Kindergarten Children
in the High and Low Reading Groups**

Variables	Reading Group	
	High	*Low*
Source of Household Income		
☐ Job of household head	7	4
☐ Social Security, ADC	2	3
☐ None listed	3	5
Household Head		
☐ Both parents	4	4
☐ Mother alone	8	6
☐ Female guardian	0	2
Telephone in Home		
☐ Yes	10	5
☐ No	2	7
Sex		
☐ Boy	3	12
☐ Girl	11	5

N = 31 for sex variable; N = 24 for three other variables

Source: Carol S. Talbert, "The Weeding-Out Process: The Relation Between Black American English and Educational Achievement," mimeographed, 1972, p. 50.

Table IV

**Comparison of Teacher Ranking of First-Grade Pupils
with Sex of the Child**

Pupil Ranking	Sex of Child	Pupil Ranking	Sex of Child
1	F	15	M
2	M	16	M
3	F	17	M
4	F	18	F
5	M	19	M
6	F	20	M
7	F	21	F
8	M	22	F
9	F	23	M
10	F	24	F
11	M	25	M
12	M	26	F
13	F	27	M
14	M	28	M

$N = 28$

Source: Carol S. Talbert, "The Weeding-Out Process: The Relation Between Black American English and Educational Achievement," mimeographed, 1972, p. 56.

negative answer to this question, since both the girls and boys who displayed aggressive and dominant behavior were the teacher's star pupils. Patricia, Sheila, James, and Gerry (whose behavior as teacher's helpers was described earlier) were, on the whole, confident, outspoken, and aggressive rather than stereotypically ladylike. While Patricia and Sheila could also behave in a saccharine manner with the teacher when the situation called for it, they could be very rough and mean with the rest of the children in other circumstances and then switch to being coy. When the teacher left the room or assigned helpers while she was present, these preferred children, both girls and boys, showed a marked degree of bullying behavior, engaging in loud talk, kicking of other children, and other aggressive acts. Inasmuch as the teacher failed to stop this behavior when she saw it occurring, it would be hard to agree with the notion that the teachers preferred girls because they were sweet and ladylike or boys because their behavior was girlish in the usual sense of the word.

Several of the boys who were in the low group on the periphery of the classroom activities also displayed aggressive behavior, but it certainly did not elicit positive responses from the teacher, although it was directed toward members of their own group, not toward the teacher or any of the high-ranking children. The boys on the periphery rarely approached the teacher or blurted out answers as the favored children were permitted to do. Clearly this teacher responded to "feminine" and "masculine" behavior very selectively. Still the sex of the child was a kind of predictor—albeit a somewhat weak one—of how she would rank a child in her class on the scale of prospective least to most successful.

Many of the other field observers had noted that the girls were not only singled out more frequently by their teachers as doing well but that girls generally received more preferential treatment than boys. Mark Schoepfle, who had also made observations in the kindergarten Talbert studied, made the following observation:

The teacher was never observed offering tactile reinforcement to a boy for any reason, whereas she frequently did so for girls—sometimes for no reason on the girl's part. That the pupils appreciated this fact was evident in the girls' frequent advances to touch her, sometimes merely in passing, while the boys always kept their distance. This difference could be seen not only in noncontent interaction (such as while the children were lining up for recess) but in content teaching, as when a girl made a correct response to a question. In these instances the girl was often hugged while the boy was given only a verbal response.[3]

The teachers were perfectly aware that the girls received more of their attention than the boys, with the exception of those boys they had to discipline repeatedly. The teachers were frank about this in their conversations with the researchers: "The boys are left alone. Girls, we watch after; boys, we don't." "Most of the teachers are teaching the girls." That the girls tended to be less disruptive and generally seemed to conform more to the teachers' demands was also recognized by the teachers. "Boys are rougher than girls" was a standard statement made by teachers when discussing discipline problems.

The influence on teacher preference exerted by the family background of a child was also explored by Talbert in her study of the first-grade class.[4] Since much of the content of the morning's Show-and-Tell material contributed by the children revolved around their experiences at home, it was rather easy for the teacher to become acquainted with the family life of each child. As has been mentioned earlier, the teacher could also get some information about the financial condition and composition of the families from the school records. However, this information was not necessarily reliable. For instance, a child's mother might have listed a father in the home who was very seldom there or she might have declined to list a father or another male who was frequently in the home. Taking the records at face value, it is shown in Table V that nine of the high children and seven of the low came from two-parent homes. The children from two-parent families were, therefore, about equally distributed between the highs and lows. But when the family composition was crosstabulated with the sex of the child, it turned out, as shown on Table VI, that only one of the six boys in the high group came from a one-parent home.

In this class, therefore, there was less of a chance for a boy whose school records indicated that he lacked a father in the home to be ranked by the teacher in the high group. Since the listing of father absence or presence could easily have been inaccurate, there was no necessary relationship between a father's actual presence in the home and the teacher's ranking of these first graders. Of course, the significant point was whether the reported presence or absence of a father in the home influenced a teacher's evaluation of a child's prospects for school success.

Although the various investigations of the correlates of teacher preference were never conclusive, the findings did suggest that social status and sex played a role in the judgments teachers made about the academic potential of their students. Classroom observations clearly supported the conclusion that teacher favoritism existed and that it was more patterned than capricious. For the most part, the teachers being observed had been teaching in the schools for many years and had developed well-established ways of conducting their classrooms. It was a regular practice for them to select potential high and low achievers early in the term according to some kind of model—one which seemed to consist of a set of behavioral traits differentiating between those who would make it and those who would not. These were not so much personality traits of the child as they were kinds of behavior displayed in the school context. According to speculation based on our observations, the children preferred by their teachers had identifiable ways of acting while at school. There were three which were the most important and they were closely interrelated. The first was what we called teachability, the second was adaptability to bureaucratic school norms, and the third was being middle class or showing potential for becoming middle class in attitudes, values, appearances, and goals.

Teachability

Our observations suggested that in the eyes of the teachers, some of the behavioral traits strongly associated with teachability were verbal skills. Considered by the teachers as especially critical to a child's school performance, these verbal skills were of several specific kinds. Among them was, first, a demonstration of some early signs of aptitude and ability in reading and writing—skills which are known to be related to, among other things, motor skills, auditory discrimination, social maturity, and familiarity with the grammar of the language being read and written.

In the first-grade class in which the teacher was asked to rank her 28 pupils in order of potential success in school, there was an almost perfect correlation between her ranking of the pupils and their mastery of reading. As seen in Table VII the teacher followed the rankings in reading skills unerringly in her evaluation of the potential success of each student, with the exception of placing one girl from the middle reading group ahead of the last boy in the high reading group.

A second significant verbal skill for a child to possess was some fluency in speaking Standard English (in contrast to Black English) and some evidence of ease in learning more of it. For many of the

Table V

**Comparison of Family Composition and Teacher Ranking
of First-Grade Pupils**

Pupil Ranking	Two-Parent Home	Pupil Ranking	Two-Parent Home
1	X	15	
2	X	16	
3		17	
4		18	X
5	X	19	X
6	X	20	
7	X	21	X
8	X	22	X
9	X	23	
10		24	
11	X	25	
12	X	26	X
13		27	X
14		28	X

$N = 28$

Source: Carol S. Talbert, "The Weeding-Out Process: The Relation Between Black American English and Educational Achievement," mimeographed, 1972, p. 56.

children who did not ordinarily speak much Standard English at home, learning to understand the Standard English spoken by the teacher in the classroom and the written English in the textbooks and other materials involved much new and difficult learning. They were confronted with the complex tasks of acquiring an additional grammar, one with different expressions of tense, number, syntax, and phonology. In order to read their textbooks and speak Standard English in the classroom, these children had to learn to perceive sounds which had not been actively functional in their speech even though they had heard them previously on television and elsewhere.

Table VI

Teacher Ranking of Children in High and Low Groups in First Grade Compared with Sex and Family Composition

Teacher Ranking	Type of Home	
	Two-Parent Home	*One-Parent Home*
High 50%	4 females 5 males	4 females 1 male
Low 50%	4 females 4 males	1 female 5 males

$N = 28$

Source: Carol S. Talbert, ''The Weeding-Out Process: The Relation Between Black American English and Educational Achievement,'' mimeographed, 1972, p. 56.

They had to acquire novel word endings and strange copula forms as well. In fact, they had to enlarge their phonological structures with almost twice the number of vowel phones. Thus, while they were struggling to learn to read and write, they were at the same time almost doubling the vowel phones that were new to them.

The teachers expected the children to use Standard English immediately in their recitations and reading even though many of them were just beginning to learn to use a great many of the new sounds and forms of Standard English. In the first-grade class studied by Talbert, the teacher disliked hearing the children use certain Black English forms and tried to eliminate them from the children's speech. The more a child used them, the more the teacher considered that child a low achiever. These judgments about the intellectual and moral attributes of the children who spoke Black English

Table VII

**Comparison of Reading Group and Teacher Ranking
in a First-Grade Classroom**

Teacher Ranking of Student	Reading Group	Teacher Ranking of Student	Reading Group
1	H	15	H
2	H	16	M
3	H	17	M
4	H	18	M
5	H	19	M
6	H	20	M
7	H	21	L
8	H	22	L
9	H	23	L
10	H	24	L
11	H	25	L
12	H	26	L
13	M	27	L
14	M	28	L

H = high reading group; M = middle reading group; L = low reading group
$N = 28$

Source: Carol S. Talbert, "The Weeding-Out Process: The Relation Between Black American English and Educational Achievement," mimeographed, 1972, p. 63.

all the time were probably not made consciously by the teacher. But as is common with other listeners to perceived "low status" language and "confused grammar," the teachers' reactions were very negative, even though they themselves often juxtaposed Standard and Black English, as is illustrated by this teacher's instructions to her class: "Now, I repeat, class, turn your books—stop runnin' yo' mouf', girl—to page 20."

A child's ability to alternate easily, correctly, and appropriately between Standard English and Black English was a third verbal skill considered desirable by the teachers. They themselves changed their speech according to the kinds of messages they were trying to convey to their students. When they were admonishing, praising, or just getting the students' attention, the teachers' speech was more like Black English, that is, more familiar, intimate, and egalitarian. They used Standard English to give directions, repeat questions, and convey information about the lessons, that is, in contexts that were more impersonal, unemotional, and formal. In the first grade studied by Talbert, the six children who were the stars, the best readers, and the most intimate with the teacher, were expert at following the teacher's lead in changing from one form to the other. Their facility at code-switching was one of the behavioral traits that appeared to endear them to the teacher.

Adaptability to School Norms

Schooling was an experience that seemed to reward those children who most readily conformed to the social order established by the school bureaucracy. The schools were more bearable places for those children who allowed their individuality and autonomy to be shaped to the constraints of the classroom and the rest of the institution.

Some of the children seemed to respond more willingly than others to the admonitions printed across the tops of the posters decorating the front wall of one first-grade classroom: "Sit Nice and Straight," "Don't Talk," "Raise Your Hand," "Don't Chew Gum," "Do Your Best Work," "Take Care of Yourself," "Be Happy," and "Smile." Although these slogans were not necessarily followed all the time by the high achievers who were the teacher's pets, they incorporated quite well how the teacher wished the students to behave most of the time. The stars participated in classroom activities, followed directions well, and gave correct answers, and although they were given much more freedom to bend the rules than the rest of the children, their teacher would curb them when they went too far. The pets were adept at responding to their teacher's ways of conducting her class and her need to keep order. On their own level, they possessed an almost uncanny grasp of how the bureaucracy worked.

The girls in the ghetto schools like girls in other American schools generally conformed more readily to the requirements of school bureaucracy than the boys. Most of them were not trouble-makers and were easier for the teachers to manage, at least in the early grades. In a sense, the teachers took advantage of the girls' greater willingness to submit to their teachers' authority. The girls who were classed as low achievers were often either neglected and ignored or forced to follow the letter of the law in their classroom behavior. Girls were expected to be quiet, orderly, and pleasant and to obey the teacher's instructions even when this might prevent them from learning the lesson being taught at the moment:

Lilly stands up out of her seat. Mrs. Caplow asks Lilly what she wants. Lilly makes no verbal response to the question. Mrs. Caplow then says rather firmly to Lilly, "Sit down." Lilly does. However, Lilly sits down sideways in the chair in order to see the writing on the blackboard. Mrs. Caplow instructs Lilly "to turn around and put your feet under the table." This Lilly does. Now she is facing directly away from the teacher and the blackboard where the teacher is demonstrating how to print the letter "O."[5]

When Lilly obeyed the seating rule, she was virtually cut off from participating in the lesson. The teacher forced her to sit with her back to the blackboard and acted as though she were perfectly justified in doing so because Lilly had broken the seating rule.

Being Middle Class

There was a considerable economic and social gap between the teachers and many of their students. In fact, in some of the schools located in impoverished areas, the teachers and the rest of the school staff constituted a middle-class corps of professionals whose lives outside of their work were spent at great distance from their lower-class clientele. In some of the schools there were a few children from families who were closer to the social status of the teachers and, like them, a number of these families were upwardly mobile. Children from these backgrounds were always among the stars.

The teachers' own backgrounds were quite varied—ranging all the way from rural poor to urban blue collar and substantial middle class—but they shared a common set of beliefs about the mobility system in the United States which they tried to pass on to the students. They believed that entry into mainstream America was a good thing to strive for and that it was possible to accomplish; that the rewards of success were material things—money, a "nice home" in a "good neighborhood," a car, and other evidences of a comfortable, even affluent, life style; that formal education was not only a good thing in and of itself, but was the critical if not the only means of achieving upward mobility.

The teachers felt that their work was socially important in great part because they were in a position to pass on these beliefs to the students and to help give some of them the start they needed to climb the ladder to middle-class success.

The stories and songs taught in the classrooms often contained themes about advancement through education.[6] "Busy Betty" and "Lazy Betty" were popular songs with such morals. Characteristic of the attempts to encourage the children to associate material success with education were the displays on the bulletin boards. For example, in the front display case at the entrance to one school building were two posters, the first showing two very poorly dressed black children with the question "Who am I?" printed across the bottom, the second showing the same two children very nicely dressed carrying signs saying, "I am Somebody—I am courteous, ambitious, honest, neat, respectful and studious." A third poster in the same display case pictured two college students in academic gowns, a black male and a white blond female, looking up at a ladder to a cloud. On the cloud were a color TV, a car, a boat, a pot of gold, a ranch-style house, and a large stack of cash. Lettered across the top was the question, "Can you climb this ladder?" The ladder between the two students was drawn to spell the word "Education" and across the bottom of the poster was the sentence, "This School Can Help."

Later in the fall the displays changed with the seasonal holidays. On one bulletin board two witches, who were white and blond, were each stirring a pot. The first pot was labeled "Study," the second, "Hard Work," and beneath them was the caption, "The

Right Formula for Success." Another poster pictured an Indian on his knees making smoke signals. Below the fire were the words "Heap Good Rules." On each puff of smoke a rule was written: "Always walk in the halls," "Be kind to other children," "Wait quietly at the fountains," and "Play safely on the playground." On another display the red letters at the top stated "You Can" and at the bottom of the board continued with "Start Now." In the middle was an article from *Ebony* magazine giving an account of the successful career of a black man from Texas who had been making cowboy boots for forty years.

A "Peanuts" cartoon strip was pinned up on another bulletin board. In the first frame, Charlie Brown and Lucy were standing outside a school. Charlie Brown stated, "I hate school." In the second frame, Lucy responded, "Good grief, Charlie Brown, school is what you make it." In the third frame, Lucy added, "Why if you are neat, clean and polite and if you study hard in class and play hard at recess, school can be great." Fourth frame: Charlie Brown, "Maybe she is right, maybe it is up to me."

The teachers recognized that some of the children were more prepared than others either by background or inclination to respond to the teachers' efforts to ready their pupils for upward mobility. For example, when role playing was used by one kindergarten teacher to show her pupils how to act properly at the dinner table, a boy from table 2 did not pass muster:

The students, acting the roles of mother, father, and daughter, are all from Table 1. The boy playing the son is from Table 2. At the small dinner table set up in the center of the classroom, the four children are supposed to be sharing with each other what they have done during the day—the father at work, the mother at home, and the two children at school. The Table 2 boy makes few comments. (In real life he has no father and his mother is supported by ADC funds.) The teacher comments, "I think that we are going to have to let Milt (Table 1) be the new son. Sam, why don't you go and sit down. Milt, you seem to be the one who would know what a son is supposed to do at the dinner table. You come and take Sam's place."[7]

Indeed, some of the children would already "know what a son is supposed to do at the dinner table." They gave evidence of this in their middle-class conduct and attitudes which served as behavioral indicators to which the teachers were attuned. In those schools where none of the families were even marginally middle class, the teachers spotted those children who showed signs of having middle-class aspirations by their dress, their manners, and their speech. When such children entered school, the teachers and the rest of the school staff were poised to help them along the road to success. Since in the staff's judgment there were too many children to prepare all of them for this upward climb and many could never make it anyway, the teachers concentrated on those children who like themselves were good prospects for becoming middle class.

The teachers possessed a kind of mental template that guided them in their choices. They nurtured the Brahmins who in turn were allowed to dominate the less-promising children—the no-bodies destined not to experience enough satisfaction in school to motivate them to persevere when everything, including the educational system, was stacked against them. Although the schools were forced to acknowledge a child's existence and accept him as a pupil, there was no attempt by anybody to force a teacher to invest her time and talent in a high-risk child. There was no assurance that a child would be taught just because he was admitted as a pupil.

Notes

1. Carol S. Talbert, "The Weeding-Out Process: The Relation Between Black American English and Educational Achievement," mimeographed, 1972, p. 35.

2. See Ray C. Rist, *The Urban School: A Factory for Failure* (Cambridge: The MIT Press, 1973), pp. 85-91.

3. Mark Schoepfle, "A Pilot Study of the Ecology of Classroom Behavior," mimeographed, 1968, p. 12.

4. Carol S. Talbert, "The Weeding-Out Process," pp. 64-146.

5. Ray C. Rist, *The Urban School*, pp. 161-62.

6. See Ray C. Rist, "The Socialization of the Ghetto Child into the Urban School System," Ph.D. dissertation, 1970, pp. 163-64.

7. Ray C. Rist, "Student Social Class and Teacher Expectations: The Self-Fulfilling Prophecy in Ghetto Education," *Harvard Educational Review* 40 (August 1970), p. 424.

CHAPTER
5 The Home and School Lockstep

*It really is the home that holds the key to whether or
not the child learns . . . . No matter what happens in
the classroom, the home is what really affects whether
the child learns. You can have the best teacher in the
world, but if the home life is miserable, the child is
not going to learn anything.*[1]
—Kindergarten teacher in a ghetto school

No one would dispute the assertion that the home is the crucial
learning milieu of the preschool child. Once a child enters school,
however, another setting is added as a site for his educational
experience. At this juncture, home and school mix and meld in the
person of the student, although in the inner-city schools being
studied the adult actors, that is, the teacher and the parents, seldom
cross paths. Even so, the influences of home and school on the
child's learning are inextricable.

One way of understanding how the child learns in these two
environments might be to know the interrelationship between them
rather than attempting to separate them into independent influences. But first it is necessary to understand the home as a place of
learning. To do this, it was decided that members of the field staff
would visit some of the children in their homes periodically while at
the same time they would continue to watch the interaction between
the teachers and these same children in the classroom.

The method of choosing the children to be observed in their
homes was important. Instead of using some measure, such as
social class, I.Q., school records, or a group of such indicators, as a

means of identifying children who were representative in some way of the elementary school population, it was the teachers' own judgments of the children and their potential which served as the basis for the sample of students. Each kindergarten teacher made the selection, according to her own criteria, of two pupils who would do well in school and two others who would do poorly. These children were studied intensively in their homes and in their classrooms as well.

The purpose of following these particular children into their homes was to compare what happened to them at home with what happened to them at school. It was hoped that the other side of the coin of teacher preference would be exposed for examination, and that seeing this other side would give some hints about what kinds of family life produced children likely to succeed or fail in these schools—which children the teacher would pick as bound for success or failure.

In attempting to study these children in their homes, a number of difficulties were encountered. The greatest problem was the irregularity of the routines of the family members, or at least what was viewed as irregularity by the research team members in the field. For example, one youngster's mother worked a swing shift in a hospital, so the child was rarely at home on school afternoons, but spent her time during her mother's absence with either her grandmother or one of two aunts. Sometimes she "slept over" with them. In the case of one of the boys, the observer was repeatedly unable to locate him by going to his address; first the address given in school records turned out to be incorrect; then no one was at home when the researcher went to the correct address. At last the researcher met the child's mother by walking home with the child after school one day.

Once an initial contact had been made with a family, there were a number of factors which interfered with ensuring that the families would be at home at the time of the appointments or the visits. The absence of telephones in many of the homes was one hindrance. Sometimes the adults forgot an appointment or were suddenly called back to the job, or a shift was changed, and so on. In one case, the living conditions themselves made meetings difficult. The rather disturbed mother of one child was fearful of meeting the observer in her tiny, cluttered apartment; for some time she insisted that she and the observer stay in the hallway and talk while the child slept upstairs on the couch. On the other hand, meetings with the families of children where the mother had some higher education were relatively easy to arrange. No disjunction in time and space was encountered. The families lived at the addresses given and were at home when they said they would be.

When an attempt was made to penetrate ghetto life from the outside as contrasted with growing up or living in it, it had to be done slowly. Some pretesting of the nonparticipatory method of observation in elementary school children's homes demonstrated some of the difficulties ahead.[2] It became clear that there would be no easy answer to the question of how the home prepared the child to be received as a student in these schools. Wrapped together in a tight and scrambled bundle were the cognitive, emotional, and interactional characteristics of each home, making their profound imprint on the child who was sent to school for an education. In the hopes of sorting out some of these characteristics, observations of two children, Rachel Potter and David Smith, were undertaken as a trial run. Rachel and David were both outgoing and alert when first observed in kindergarten. The families of both children were poor and lived in the same housing project, but there were marked differences in the ways the parents and other members of the household related to the children, as the following descriptions of the two families showed:

The Potter Family

Rachel Potter was one of five children who lived with their mother and father in an urban renewal high-rise housing project. Mr. Potter was an unskilled worker who spent his free time at home, but remained rather aloof from the children. On the other hand, Mrs. Potter seemed deeply involved in the children's lives. She was affectionate with them, but at the same time handled them in a firm and clearheaded manner. Active herself in a religious movement, she involved the rest of the family in study periods devoted to the ideology of the sect. A good deal of religious literature was always around the house.

The five Potter children were very competitive with each other, but they obeyed their mother when she intervened in order to maintain fair play with such admonitions as, "Give Pam a chance, Rachel. It's not your turn." The children often played at doing schoolwork. In fact, television watching seemed to be subordinated to playing school.

The Potters' apartment consisted of four rooms, a combination living room and kitchen-dining room plus three bedrooms. The furniture was arranged so that there was a clear distinction between the living room and dining-kitchen areas. The living room was furnished to present the family "front" while the rear rooms were drab and bare. All the rooms were kept neat and clean. Each of the children had a permanent bedroom assignment and only the members of the immediate family lived in the apartment.

The Smith Family

The household in which David Smith lived was held together by his illiterate 59-year-old great-grandmother, Mrs. Thompson. In addition to David, his four sisters, and Mrs. Thompson, three other people lived in the apartment with some regularity: James, the children's violent, unstable 35-year-old great-uncle who was Mrs. Thompson's son; 15-year-old Josephine, whom Mrs. Thompson called her daughter; and Thomas, another of Mrs. Thompson's grandchildren. David's mother and father were separated. Neither lived in the apartment with their five children, but the children's mother, who was described as "wild" by Mrs. Thompson, was an occasional visitor in the home as was another of Mrs. Thompson's daughters.

Mrs. Thompson was almost entirely dependent on public agencies for financial support. Although the children's mother received ADC checks, she did not contribute anything to the support of the children. But the great-grandmother often said that she could not bear to go on living if she did not have her grandchildren to take care of. She acted well disposed toward them, but her contacts with them were mostly quite impersonal. Indeed, when speaking about the children in their presence, she often belittled them and herself as well. Her communication with the children was infrequent and limited largely to commands and admonitions. She was unable to get them to respond to her discipline and seemed to have little authority over them or respect from them and the other members of the household. She had suffered a stroke, her vision was poor, and she was somewhat confused, but far from mentally ill.

David and his sisters spent most of their time at home watching television. Although they were very competitive with each other while playing, they were never seen playing school or doing any schoolwork at home. They had to contend with their Uncle James who was a punitive and threatening figure in their everyday lives.

The apartment had the same physical layout as the Potters' but it was kept very differently. It was dirty and always in disarray. The furniture was moved around frequently. No clear distinction was made between the living room and dining room-kitchen areas. The only person who had a fixed sleeping place was Uncle James who had his own room and his own television set.

It would seem as if the stage were set for some logical consequences of these contrasting childrearing environments: David's performance in school would be miserable from the beginning. He would never have a chance from the start, considering his home life. On the other hand, Rachel's prospects would be brighter since her family was a stable one and had many middle-class ways, even though the family income was low enough to qualify them for a public housing project.

To compare how the two children performed in their first two years of school, an observer monitored their classrooms and coded their responses to questions directed at them by their kindergarten and first-grade teachers. In kindergarten David gave the right answers about half the time compared to Rachel's correct responses more than three-quarters of the time. Their social behavior was very different: David showed leadership and was helpful with his classmates but at times was inattentive, acted up, and neglected his work. Rachel was never observed doing any of these things. The kindergarten teacher struck David several times for his behavior.

During the summer between kindergarten and first grade, David began disappearing from home for many hours. He was beaten harshly for doing this by his father who was located by the family specifically for this purpose. He was also beaten by his great-uncle who frequently created violent scenes in the household.

In the fall of first grade, the school principal whipped David for urinating in the playground. But things took a different turn in his first-grade classroom. His teacher, Mrs. Trask, expressed much more interest in him than his kindergarten teacher had and told the observer that she planned to help him perform at the best possible level in her class. His performance did improve. In fact, David's responses to his first-grade teacher's questions were correct more often than Rachel's (70 percent right answers for David compared with 55 percent for Rachel). But David continued to be less attentive in class than Rachel and began sucking his thumb occasionally.

In the midwinter grading period, David and Rachel received identical marks on their report cards. Mrs. Trask compared the children and their prospects: "The reason for Rachel's success in school is more one of control and discipline than of capacity. With drive and push Rachel will be consistently good. She takes the time to think. David has it, too, but he's not so controlled and he's getting into trouble in the schoolyard. He's becoming a behavior problem. He's very aggressive and is basically a tough little boy. And he won't study his words."

From these preliminary observations of two children at home and at school, several impressions about the sources of potential success or failure in their performance at school emerged. There was the warning that the child's fate at school came out of an exceedingly complex universe, even though the child was still so young and impressionable. Within this complexity, the school system, with its many and diverse actors and characteristics, operated as only one influence on the children's lives. But it was obviously a large and crucial part. It was also somewhat unpredictable because of such chance factors as which teachers would be assigned to which students. David's kindergarten teacher had struck him for acting up and the principal beat him for urinating in the schoolyard, but his first-grade teacher took a greater interest in him than his kindergarten teacher. This pointed out both the harsh treatment awaiting this kind of youngster at the hands of the school as well as the discontinuity of such treatment in the hands of a more understanding teacher.

The school and its particular culture as it interacted with the consequences of a child's emotional and cognitive experiences at home, however, seemed to make certain kinds of specific demands upon the students. It drew a line between those children whom the school would accept as candidates for their attention and those they would not. Whether David, for example, would be able to develop his potential undoubtedly depended on many factors in this intersection of the home and school environment. Some of the most important of these were the ways in which the home life of the child—his parents and guardians, his siblings, other members of the household, and his friends—affected how he would be regarded and treated at school. Would he fit one of the acceptable models? As Mrs. Trask so aptly put it, "The reason for Rachel's success in school is more one of control and discipline than of capacity. . . . David has it, too, but he's not so controlled and he's getting into trouble. . . ." What David brought to school apparently was getting him into trouble and making the chances for his getting an education negligible, even though he "has it, too," as Mrs. Trask expressed it.

The research team shared the view widely held by the teachers that the child's experience at home was critical to his success or failure in school. However, they differed from the teachers in their formulation of the relationship between the home and learning. Most of the teachers thought that the home life of the children had either a positive or negative effect on whether they would learn and that the teachers could do little to alter the influence of the family upon the child. They seemed to believe this in an almost fatalistic way.

The research team, on the other hand, viewed all the elements in the child's life as interacting so that the outcome of schooling depended on a complex of factors which were not necessarily unalterable. If one element of the child's life, for example, his experience at home, took on a largely negative significance for his schoolwork (which we might assume for the sake of argument was the situation in David's case), this might be overcome if certain factors at school were maximized, such as an improvement in teaching methods, that is, the use of some special approaches to children like David. Of course, if one such factor were maximized, it might be canceled by a negative indication in another, as in the home or peer group situation. What the research team hoped to discover was what elements in the home life of the children were responded to negatively and positively by participants in the school culture. If there were patterns of response by the school system to children coming from backgrounds with certain characteristics, it would be important to know which behavior patterns created a negative or positive response in the school system. The outcome of a child's total educational experience—including his experience at home, with his peers, and at school over time—might be improved if one element, for example, his experience at school, were maximized so that positive learning would exceed negative and result in success rather than failure.

During the months and years of visiting the children's families, the observers made detailed records of what happened in the homes of the children selected by their teachers as doing poorly and doing well. The lengthy protocols of the observations of family life recorded by the field staff were studied and analyzed. After 180 visits made in 28 homes, each lasting ordinarily about an hour and a half, it was almost overwhelmingly evident that other forces originating elsewhere in the larger system, not simply in the homes and schools of the children, had pervasive effects on this population and its institutions. It would be an egregious mistake to underrate the consequences of the social and economic marginality of this black community on the lives of the families and the children and on the schools which were supposed to educate them.

Out of the raw data about the homes and schools of inner-city children, many impressions emerged. We concentrated mostly on the general question of what similarities existed between a child's relationship with his parents and his relationship with his teachers. We looked at the nature and frequency of child/adult interaction and at the amount of negative and positive responses between these pairs.

Making use of the naturalistic observations of family life was of course a difficult task and we cannot pretend that all of the data was analyzed systematically. In the case studies of the families which follow we have drawn on papers written by the field staff who visited the families of the children periodically over considerable lengths of time. These observers knew the children well, both at home and at school. The case studies are meant to be suggestive of the variety and richness of the children's experiences in their homes. The accounts include descriptions of the general living conditions of the families, and of the children's parents, guardians, and other members of the household and how they interact on their home territory. Particular attention is given to how the children spend their time, what kind of information is exchanged in the family, and what sorts of rewards and punishments the children's behavior elicits from their parents. In the case studies of the six families, two children selected by their teachers as doing well and five children as doing poorly are presented in their home surroundings. Following each case study, a short discussion of how the youngster is treated at school tries to suggest how each child fails or suceeds at filling the model of a teachable child.

Lynn Ames—A Child Doing Poorly

Lynn Ames's family lives about two blocks from School 4 in an apartment building which, like many others on the block, is run down and dilapidated.[3] Lynn has two older brothers and three sisters ranging in age from eight to 12. The apartment has only two bedrooms and the six children have to sleep in two small beds in one of the two bedrooms. Both of the parents work full time at night. Mr. Ames, who has finished two years of college, is a welder in an assembly division of the Ford Motor Company; Mrs. Ames, a high school graduate, is a nurse's aide in a nearby hospital. They spend most of the day sleeping, during which time the children are left free to do whatever they choose. Many times the children are locked out of the house so that their parents can rest. The general housekeeping of the apartment is neglected. The living room is littered with beer cans; dust and dirty sheets cover the couch; the bedrooms have clothes scattered on the floor; the unmade beds have dirty linen or none at all; the bedroom windows are covered with tattered sheets. The children's clothes are usually dirty, wrinkled, and torn and their hair is uncombed. However, Mrs. Ames keeps her own clothes in good condition.

Most of the meals are prepared by either Mr. Ames or the oldest girl, Charlene, who is 10 years old. Their breakfast usually consists of rice and bacon or rice alone. Since no lunch is prepared, the children get hungry during the day and often go to the store to buy cookies or ice cream with small change they receive for doing odd jobs in the neighborhood. The children frequently argue over food or beg for food from the one who happens to have some. Unless

Mrs. Ames makes provision for lunch, which she seldom does, Lynn gets very little to eat. For example, on one afternoon the children were sitting outside after Mrs. Ames had gone to the election polls, having said nothing to the children about food for lunch before she left:

Claudia told Lynn that she had some doughnuts inside the house that the man from the bakery had given her. Claudia went inside and got the doughnuts from under a chair in the living room. I had heard Claudia and Daniel talking about them earlier. He had told her that he was going to go and get them. She said that he couldn't because he didn't know where they were. When she took the doughnuts out of the hiding place, she gave Daniel and Lynn very small pieces, just enough for one bite. When Daniel begged for more, she gave him a half of a doughnut. Lynn begged for more too, but Claudia said, "No." Gerald, who is older than the other three, came in. He told Claudia to give him one. He didn't beg like the others, he just demanded that she give him one. After she gave him only half a doughnut, he tried to snatch more but he seemed a little reluctant since I was there. He looked over at me once or twice. He then told Claudia softly that he was going to "get her" and he walked out. Charlene then came upstairs eating a pint of ice cream. Daniel and Lynn immediately ran over to her and begged her for some and she finally gave Lynn one spoonful and went back outside.

Lynn never gives up asking for a share of someone's snack even through she is rarely given any:

All of the children came to the front where Claudia was eating some corn-on-the-cob; Lynn complained to me that Claudia wouldn't give her any. I'm sure Mrs. Ames must have heard this but she said nothing. Claudia just laughed and told Lynn that she could get some herself if she wanted to. After Claudia had eaten about half of the cob she gave the other half to her girl friend. Mrs. Ames told the children to go outside so that she could sleep.

Lynn is usually very quiet and withdrawn around the members of her family, but sometimes she succeeds at getting some attention by either provoking them or running errands for them:

Lynn was about to play with the neighbor's hula hoop when a slightly larger boy who was with her brother took it away from her. He played with it until he got tired and decided to leave. Meanwhile Lynn and Claudia sat down. When the boy left, Lynn quickly picked the hoop up from the ground where he had thrown it and began to play. Claudia tried to take it away from her but when Lynn fought for it and hollered, Claudia sat down. Claudia came over and tried to take it again. Lynn screamed and the hoop rolled away. Claudia took the hoop and paid no attention to Lynn.

Lynn is especially quiet and withdrawn around her mother, and the other children in the family also keep their distance from their mother. A typical kind of interaction between the children and Mrs. Ames is illustrated by what happened on a summer day:

Mrs. Ames had been working in the kitchen and came to the front where I was sitting, saying she had to take a break now. She told Claudia to take an old paper bag and put it in the trash and Lynn to get the extension cord. (They both obeyed immediately.) Roy came in and went into the bedroom without speaking. Mrs. Ames called him and asked where he had been. At first he did not respond and then he said "Nowhere"; however, he didn't say this until Mrs. Ames told him that I was out in the living room. He then came out and said "Nowhere." She said that he had to have been some-where and he finally admitted that he had been at Sears. She asked what he was doing there and he said he was with an aunt. She asked whether the aunt was shopping and who she was with and Roy said that she was with "herself" and didn't have any packages. He said that she bought a hot dog for him and Mrs. Ames asked whether she brought him home and he said, "No." Lynn came over and got on the couch and Mrs. Ames told her im-mediately to get on the floor because she was dirty. Claudia and Lynn went out and Roy started to go outside. Mrs. Ames told him to pull the fan closer and go see whether the man was still in the back. (There was a man repairing the latch on the door.) Roy went in the back after he pulled the fan up but never returned to tell Mrs. Ames whether or not the man was still there. She got on the couch and closed her eyes.

Abruptness, rather than any kind of explanatory communication, characterized whatever interchange occurred between the children and their mother:

Charlene came in with two cousins from Memphis who were about Charlene's age. They were staying with their grandmother and would be visiting for the weekend. They didn't say anything when they arrived until Mrs. Ames finally asked Charlene where she had been. She said that she had been over at her grandmother's.

On another day when the observer was visiting the Ames's:

> Someone knocked on the door and Mrs. Ames who had come back into the bedroom from the back was lying on the bed. She did not move. Lynn ran down and came up with a clothing catalogue which Charlene had brought. Charlene did not come up at this time. Lynn took the catalogue to Mrs. Ames who then got up and walked over to the dresser, saying nothing. She got something and sat back down on the bed. Charlene came in about five minutes later. She said to me that Claudia was still at her aunt's. She spoke to me and peeped into the bedroom; however, Mrs. Ames said nothing and Charlene left in about half a minute.

There is a prevailing air of indifference about personal relationships in the home. It is usual for Mrs. Ames not to talk to the children except to tell them to do something for her or to sit down when they are too active or noisy. With the exception of orders and reprimands, then, almost no verbal communication occurs between Mrs. Ames and the children. Most of the time she simply ignores them and they seem to react to her in the same way.

Lynn Ames at School: An Isolate

Lynn's teachers agree that she is shy, but not incapable of learning. However, in class they do not expect her to respond to questions or to participate in other classroom activities. Since she is not included in either the group of children who are taught or those who make trouble and are punished, she is usually excluded from the teacher network of relations. She has been pushed to the periphery of the class and is ignored by the teacher and the children. She is one of the nobodies. Her life space at school is much like that at home.

Emily Burns—A Child Doing Well

Emily Burns lives with her mother and grandparents in the latter's apartment along with seven other members of the family.[4] Emily's mother, Ann, was divorced after being married only one month to a man who is not Emily's father. Ann is one of eight children ranging in age from 10 to 26, six of whom still live at home. Emily's Aunt Martha who lives with them is also a divorcee and has two children; one is five and the other is almost a year old. Thus there are 11 people living in an apartment which has only four rooms plus a kitchen and bath. Three of the rooms are bedrooms. Mr. and Mrs. Burns have a room alone downstairs; upstairs, there are two other rooms containing five beds. Emily sleeps with her mother in a small bed, and the others are spread out among the four remaining beds.

The apartment and furniture are in generally poor condition but the living room and kitchen are usually kept in a kind of cluttered order. The rooms are very crowded with people and possessions, including a television, a radio, a record player that is out of order, and quite a few books and magazines. Emily had subscriptions to a book club during the school year and received the *Weekly Reader Magazine* in the summer months.

Emily's mother finished high school and one year of teachers' college; she was in the army for two years and was recently employed as a nurse's aide. She has plans to study to become a registered nurse on a grant from a community development agency after which she expects to leave the city and take Emily with her.

Mrs. Burns worked as an elevator operator until she recently quit her job to make preparations for moving. Mr. Burns, who has held many different jobs, was unemployed for a year until he was offered a management position in a company where he had previously worked. Expecting to have more money and a car, the family intends to move to a place more suited to their needs. Emily, who was taken care of by her grandmother while her mother was in the service, will remain with her grandmother while her mother lives in the nurses' dormitory during her training.

Emily is an active and socially adept child of six. She receives a great deal of attention at home and is given an abundance of toys:

Emily brought a doll to show me. It came with a tricycle and a horse, both of which the doll could ride. Emily gave a demonstration. Ann said that she had gotten the doll last week and Emily had played with it for about three days and was tired of it until today when she had gotten it out again. Emily said that she wanted another kind of doll she had seen on television. Ann then asked her how many dolls she had now and she said, "Eight." Ann said that she was going to "pitch" some of the old ones and Emily said that she was thinking about the same thing. Ann then said to me that Emily didn't want to play with her dolls any more because they were supposedly too old.

Although Ann works at night she manages to spend her days with Emily, doing many things with her. They play games together, go to the park and to the movies, and joke a lot:

Ann then began to play with Emily, singing a commercial and holding the doll and saying, "Knock on my Norge." Emily then called Ann a Norge and Ann asked Emily if she looked like a refrigerator. Emily said, "No." Emily then asked whether the doll was a Norge and Ann said, "No, it is a Mattel." Emily then asked what Norge was and Ann replied, "A brand name telling who made it." Emily asked Ann what her brand name was (referring to Ann) and Ann said, "Burns." Emily then named a number of people, asking Ann to tell her their brand names. She did this until Ann said that that was enough.

Emily and Marvin started playing with the piece of paper containing the directions that went with the doll. Ann asked if she could see it and Emily and Marvin played with her, not giving it to her by holding it away when she reached out. They laughed and Ann pretended to be angry, folded her arms and sat back. Emily came over and sat beside her and put her arms around her. Ann said jokingly, "I'm mad," and Emily said, "I'm trying to make you feel better."

Ann encourages Emily to talk freely and ask questions which she answers readily. Emily occasionally interrupts her mother as at one point when Ann was telling the observer about some of her experiences in the army. Ann usually overlooks these interruptions and responds to Emily positively:

Emily asked where she could find a pencil and some paper because she wanted to write. Ann told her to look upstairs in the bedroom. At this time, it started to rain. Ann told Emily to go and get her bathing suit and they would go out and take a shower. Emily then said to me she had taken a shower the last time it rained. Emily asked Ann which swimming suit she wanted. Ann told her the blue one and explained to me that she wouldn't dare wear her bikini outside because the last time they had gone out, her mother knew about it before she could get in the door. She said people around the neighborhood still thought she was a child and they told her mother things before they said anything to her. Emily, Marvin, Joan's youngest son, and Ann put on their suits and went out and ran up and down the sidewalk for a while in the rain.

While Ann is permissive with Emily about interruptions, at the same time she expects her to complete her light chores, run errands around the house, and be obedient:

Emily got up and told Ann that she was going outside. Ann asked her where she was going but Emily ran out without answering. Ann then went to the door and called her sternly to ask where she was going. Emily said that she was going out to see where Fred was. However, she came back and sat down. After a few minutes, she said she was going again and Ann told her that she wasn't going to stand for that so Emily sat down. Ann then took out a book and began to read some poems to Emily.

Ann uses joking and distraction to soften her orders and is very good-humored with all the children in the household:

Mr. Burns was cooking and the children were sitting in the living room for a while. Ann teased Emily about being able to see through the dress that she had on. Emily blushed and sat down in the chair next to Ann. She had taken off her shoes and was walking around with her socks on. Ann told her to take them off because she had so much trouble getting them clean. Mrs. Burns called Emily to tell her not to put her feet on the cleanest chair in the house. When Emily went back and sat down in the same chair, Ann told her to move into another chair. Ann told her that she had something for her—a big piece of multi-colored bubble gum called psychedelic gum. Ann divided it among the children and gave Emily the largest piece, telling her that she had better not eat it all because if she did she would be angry with her. Ann took a few pieces of the gum and played with Emily, picking out some of the smaller pieces and telling her to close her eyes and she would put it in her mouth. The children laughed and Emily did, too.

Ann and Emily read together often and Ann helped Emily improve both her reading and writing skills. She bought one of the first-grade readers for her and helped her to finish it. With Ann's help, Emily learned how to embroider. In all these skills Ann was demanding about good performance:

Emily said that she had something to show me and she looked at Ann when she said this. Ann said that she could show it, but that Emily knew that her mother was angry with her. When Emily went out to get whatever it was, Ann explained that she was angry because Emily had made a mistake in her embroidery. She had been embroidering all morning and wouldn't admit that she was tired and then she finally made a wrong stitch. Emily brought out her cloth and showed it to me. The design was flowers and leaves. Ann said that if it turned out nice enough they would give it as a gift. Ann looked at Emily's embroidery and said that she thought it was pretty good.

During the summer between kindergarten and first grade, Emily attended Bible School and later went with her mother to Gainesville, Florida, by train to visit friends for two weeks. Ann encouraged Emily to participate in activities away from home and also was involved in them herself:

At about noon, Emily, Ray, Leslie and Fred came in from Bible School. Emily immediately handed Ann a note from school about the closing exercises and asked her mother if she was coming to the program. Ann said, "Yes," and spoke to each one of the other children. The note said that they should wear white or something light and Ann immediately said that she would have to buy Emily a dress and do her hair. She commented that she would have a very busy day because she would have to go shopping and do Emily's hair and then be ready for dinner and get back in time for the program. Fred and Ray said that they were in the choir program and Leslie and Emily said that they had to pray and sing.

The subject of the upcoming train trip to Gainesville was brought up frequently by Emily:

Emily said that her mother had told her that they would get a car on the train. Ann laughed and explained that it was a sleeping car. She explained how it looked, saying that it was similar to a bus but the seats were farther apart and facing each other. Emily said that she wanted to sit by the window and Ann said that both of them would be able to sit by the window.

Emily then asked Ann how much money they had to spend in Florida and Ann said, "About $100, but if Steve (one of her friends in the army) gave us $50, we'd be all right." Emily then asked, "What about the money Uncle Sam owes you?" Ann said she hadn't gotten that yet, but if she did they would be in good shape because Uncle Sam owed her over $100. Emily then asked what credit was and Ann commented, "Where do you get all those words?" and she went on to say that credit was like getting something and paying for it later. She asked Emily whether she wanted to buy something on credit and Emily said, "No," but wanted to know if she could get credit. Ann told her that she was too young. Emily asked, "What if you signed for me?" and Ann said, "Then you could get it."

Emily Burns at School: A Star

Emily's teachers like her and consider her a good student. She seems to understand most of the lessons, as indicated by the greater number of right than wrong answers she gives. An active member of the class, she volunteers frequently and always raises her hand rather than talking out. Since she usually obeys the classroom rules and does not guess at answers, the teacher rarely corrects or reprimands her. She occupies a central position among the other students, especially among the girls with whom she is something of a leader. However, unlike most of the other girls, she also associates frequently with the boys. Never appearing either anxious or uncertain on the one hand or passive on the other, she seems very stable and spontaneous in her classroom behavior.

Lilly George—A Child Doing Poorly

Lilly George is one of 11 children ranging in age from newborn to 16.[5] Her mother was born in the rural South and worked in the cotton fields from the age of eight. She had a total of about four years of formal schooling. When she was 18 she moved north to the city. She and her family are on public welfare and live in a dilapidated duplex in a slum area. Several of the children have suffered severe burns from contact with the gas stoves which are the only means of heating the house in the winter. The house is kept clean on the inside and is very sparsely furnished. Since none of the children have closets or chests in their bedrooms, their clothes are piled on the floor. There is not a single book or toy among the children's possessions.

On the researcher's first visit with the George family, there was a middle-aged man in the apartment who got up from the couch when he saw him, put a whiskey bottle in his pocket and turned his face to the wall. Several minutes later he stumbled into the kitchen and asked Mrs. George, "What the hell does this guy want here?" She replied, "He's at school; he's in Lilly's class. He's coming to find out how she's doing in school." The man said, "Well, what the shit, if you want to find out how the child's doin' you can go and talk to the teacher. There's no need of botherin' us." Mrs. George's reply was, "Aw, shut up and get out of here."

Meanwhile, Lilly was busy doing what seemed to be a school assignment, attempting to paste objects she had cut out onto a sheet of paper. When the researcher tried to talk with her, she either answered "Yassuh" or nothing at all. Her mother tried to prompt her, "Lilly, the man's talkin' to you. Now let's say sumpin' to him," but Lilly kept repeating, "Yassuh, yassuh."

On a subsequent visit, the researcher found eight of the children in the living room with their mother. She sat in her usual place on the couch holding a stick four or five feet long with which she hit the children whenever they got out of line. The living room was small enough for her to reach almost any part of it with the stick. When the researcher sat down, the children swarmed all over him. They fought and hit each other as they tried to climb on his lap, but Mrs. George did not make any attempt to stop them, even when four-year-old Joseph hit the two-year-old girl in the face and knocked her to the floor. Lilly was bashful as usual. However, when the researcher asked her whether she knew any of the school songs, she sang "Jingle Bells" all the way through with almost no mistakes.

Mrs. George was laconic in her answers to the researcher's questions and was also very short with the children, using very simple sentences such as "Boy, shut up, or I hit ya." "Girls, sit down where you are." "Shut up." "Boy, get that bread back in the kitchen." When eight-year-old Christopher went outside with Janice, his 10-year-old sister, he must have said, "Fuck you" to her, because when she came back in she said to her mother, "Christopher's out there using them bad words again; 'fu . . .' you know what." Mrs. George said, "Oh, well, have him come in here, I want to see him." Janice went to the door and shouted, "Christopher, get in here, mama wants to see you." Christopher came in and stood by the door. His mother said, "Boy, what you usin' them bad words for?'' When he did not respond, she continued, ''Boy, do you use them bad words?'' He shook his head, and his mother said, ''Sistah says you did. Don't use them bad words any more. You're not supposed to talk like that. Don't you know any better? Go over there and sit down.'' She hit him with her stick as he went toward the chair next to the stove.

The television was always going when the researcher came to the home. This day the Wednesday afternoon movie was turned on but the children—the 10 of them who were in the living room—did not seem to be paying any attention to it. However, throughout the afternoon, the children stopped whatever they were doing as soon as a commercial came on and sang along with it. Mrs. George started talking to the children about school, asking Lilly first what she did at school that day. When Lilly replied that she played in the playhouse, her mother laughed. The researcher explained that the children had been learning by playing doctor, nurse, and patient and that the playhouse had become the doctor's office. Lilly added that she got a shot from the doctor. Her mother stiffened, ''Girl, you didn't tell me about getting no shot,'' not realizing that it was a pretend shot and toy equipment until the researcher told her.

Mrs. George then asked Christopher what he had learned in school, and when he said, ''Toys,'' she said, ''Boy, we're not talking about what you do when you play. We're talking about what you do when you learn. Now you don't learn toys in school. Tell the man what you learn in school today.'' Christopher did not respond. Perceiving the anxiety of the child, the researcher said, ''Did you learn your *ABC's* today?'' and, rather excitedly, Christopher began, ''*A, B, C, D, E, F, T,*'' trailing off into a series of other letters which were out of order and pronounced unintelligibly. Lilly (who is meek and almost speechless at school) spoke up roughly to her brother, ''Christopher, boy, you don't know what you're talking about, shut up and I'll try it,'' but Lilly was even more confused. Then the four-year-old took it up, and he was still more mixed up than the others.

On this visit and during the ones that followed, the researcher decided to help the children regularly at home with their alphabet and numbers. With the three youngest school-age children on his lap, he pronounced the letters and asked the children to repeat them, going through the alphabet three times and then through the numbers from one to 20 twice. At this point, the researcher stopped, but Christopher immediately asked, "Why you stoppin'?" When the researcher replied, "Well, isn't that enough for today?" they all said, "No, tell us some more." So they started working on addition problems, one plus one equals two, and so forth, doing these drills for about 30 minutes longer. The children concentrated intensely and were very, very eager to give the answers, being distracted only when a singing commercial came on the television. Then they would break off the lesson, sing the commercial and turn back immediately to their lesson. Mrs. George sat as always at the far end of the couch watching the lesson and looking very pleased.

From time to time Mrs. George laughed at the children. For example, Lilly and Christopher had a hard time saying *Z*, pronouncing it like *C* or *T*. The researcher worked hard with them on this, but their mother and the oldest daughter continued to laugh at the children's efforts. Mrs. George asked the youngest girl to try it and she came quite close. Mrs. George was obviously pleased that the young one could do better than her older brothers and sister. Just as the researcher was about to leave that day, Mrs. George called over Christopher and said, "Christopher, you're in the second grade, can you spell your name?" and he started with a *B*. His mother ridiculed him, saying, "Boy, you're so stupid, you ought not even be in school. You're dumber than Lilly. Lilly, can you spell your name?" Lilly said, "*L-I*" and her mother started laughing, even though Lilly was right, so Lilly stopped in the middle of her name.

When the researcher came back for another visit, 16-year-old Gwendolyn had just returned from the hospital where she had given birth to a 4-pound, 8-ounce baby who was still at the hospital and in critical condition. Asked what the trouble was she said, "He's a sicklin', and there's sompin' else wrong with him." Christopher interrupted her saying, "You promised us we'd work on numbers again today," and three of the children climbed on the researcher's knees demanding more lessons. This time during the alphabet and counting, the commercials distracted the children less often and they seemed to be able to remember the letters in order and pronounce them better. Lilly counted correctly to 30, Christopher to 28, an improvement over the previous time. Four-year-old Joseph climbed up on the researcher's lap, saying that he wanted to learn, too. When Christopher pushed him away, Mrs. George said, "Boy, get out of here" and she caught Christopher across the back with a 5-foot length of electric extension cord.

Suddenly there was a loud noise outside the house. Mrs. George went outside and returned in a minute, expressing satisfaction that her oldest boy, Curtis, had gotten the best of another boy in a fight. Curtis came in with her and was sobbing, but his mother didn't pay any attention to him. Lilly said to the researcher, "There's been a fight outside" and the children resumed their lesson. But at this point, Jeff, the father of Gwendolyn's child, came in the house and caused some distraction which broke up the lesson.

On another day, the researcher engaged Mrs. George in a conversation about Lilly's experiences at kindergarten, asking her a set of six open-ended questions about how she thought Lilly liked school, what papers she brought home, and how she liked the other children in her class. Mrs. George answered with very definite opinions and with a good grasp of the work Lilly brought home, such as the exercises on mathematical sets which she described as "papers that stress things that are alike or things that are different."

At the conclusion of another session with the children on the alphabet and counting, the researcher took Lilly and two of the other children to the corner grocery store and bought them candy bars to take home, with enough to give to the children at home, but not any for their mother. The baby girl was eating her candy sitting next to her mother, when all of a sudden Mrs. George took a bite from the baby's bar. The baby let out a shriek whereupon Mrs. George grabbed Lilly's bar out of her hand and put it in the baby's mouth, saying, "Now take back the same bite I took from yours." The baby took a bite and quieted down and her mother said to the researcher, "You know, this one's so stingy, she won't give any one nothing'." Then turning to the baby she added, "Well, if you won't give me no candy, I'm not gonna give you no supper."

Lilly George at School: The Lost One

Lilly George is an exceedingly quiet child at school. In her kindergarten class which has an average attendance of about 28 children, Lilly is among the most withdrawn. She is one of the children on the periphery who rarely respond to the teacher's questions. She almost never joins the others on her own in class activities such as singing, clapping, forming circles, parading around the room, and crowding together with the other children to look at something new and interesting. Lilly's detached, inattentive, uninterested, and sometimes confused behavior and attitude in the classroom contrasts sharply with her behavior at home. After only a few visits with the Georges, the researcher saw her show alertness, interest, an ability to concentrate, and even aggressiveness.

On the very first day of school it became evident that Lilly's teacher was going to focus most of her attention on a few children and to allow those children like Lilly who were shy and withdrawn to drift. Actually this teacher seemed to be the least openly punitive of the ghetto teachers observed; she was not harsh with them, but for the most part just let children like this alone. In Lilly's case, the teacher was particularly offended by the strong smell of urine on her, but this did not mean that the teacher was a person of ill will. For example, she paid for Lilly's milk out of her own pocket throughout the school term. There is an oceanic class difference between this teacher and most of her pupils. The relatively low frequency of attention she paid to the majority of the children, including Lilly, appears to stem partly from this social distance and partly from the enormous concentration of her time on what she calls her "responsive children," one of whom is Franklin Lewis. Franklin's family moves in the same social circles as the teacher and he is in fact the only child in her class whose home she has ever visited.

Franklin Lewis—A Child Doing Well

Franklin Lewis lives with his parents and maternal grandmother in a very well furnished seven-room house in a neighborhood where his grandmother has lived since childhood.[6] Both his mother and grandmother are college graduates. His mother's degree is in special education and she works for the public school system; his grandmother taught music for many years in the public schools before retirement and still gives private piano lessons at home. She keeps house for the family as well. Mr. Lewis is head custodian at one of the schools being studied and also ushers and performs butler functions at banquets and other "fancy affairs" after hours.

Franklin is an only child and is one of the few children in the school district who attended nursery school before entering kindergarten.

As the researcher is approaching the Lewis house for the first time, Franklin is watching for him at the window and opens the door and invites him inside enthusiastically. His grandmother gets up immediately from the piano where she is giving a lesson, introduces herself, and tells the researcher how glad she is that he is working with Franklin. Mrs. Lewis comes down from upstairs, introduces herself, and explains that she had been upstairs watching TV with the mother of the children who came to the home for piano lessons. She invites the researcher into the dining room and eventually introduces the mother of the children taking lessons as a mathematics teacher in the high school. The grandmother brings refreshments from the kitchen and the women make small talk, discussing the various things they have been doing. The grandmother talks about a meeting of the League of Women Voters and encourages the other women to attend the next meeting to hear a speech by the first Negro woman elected to the Georgia Assembly. Then the two younger women discuss some problems they are having in their teaching.

Meanwhile, Franklin shows the researcher a box filled with his old school papers dating back to nursery school which he entered when he was three. Now five years old, he had started kindergarten at four which made him one of the youngest children in the class. Mrs. Lewis seems annoyed by Franklin's participation in the conversation and tries to get him to leave, "Franklin, don't show him those things. He's seen them already. What would he want to look at those things now for? We're supposed to be talking." But Franklin keeps on showing the researcher his papers and the researcher looks at them with him and discusses them.

At about 5 P.M., Mr. Lewis comes into the house and Franklin greets him with, "Hi, Fred," but there is no verbal exchange between husband and wife nor do they kiss. Nor is Mr. Lewis introduced to the researcher when they say "hello" to each other. Mrs. Lewis eventually asks her husband whether he would like a seat but he declines and goes upstairs. When he comes back down, he and his wife do not speak to each other. He sits down on the opposite side of the table from her and engages the researcher in a conversation first about football and then about the war. Suddenly Mrs. Lewis cuts into the conversation saying, "Did you see Carol Channing on TV last night?" and goes on to describe how funny she had been and how much she had enjoyed her. Meanwhile Mr. Lewis keeps on trying to make his points about the war. At last they both stop. Franklin continues to bring other things to show the researcher—more school papers, drawings, toys, and pamphlets describing his globe which is on the dining room chest, "I got the globe when my mommy bought me the encyclopedia."

When the researcher gets up to leave, Mr. Lewis is on the telephone, but he stops talking to shake hands and to express his pleasure that the researcher is interested in Franklin, adding that he hopes he will come back again to visit. Mrs. Lewis tells the researcher that she and Franklin's kindergarten teacher are good friends and are members of the same bridge club. She asks him some questions about his background, whether he is married, and so forth, and inquires whether he would like to come again. As the researcher takes his leave, she walks out on the front porch with him and Franklin comes outside, too. His mother says to him brusquely, "Franklin, get back in there. We're talking now. It's too cold here for you anyway."

On a subsequent visit with the Lewises, the researcher finds Franklin at home with the flu. He and one of his grandmother's pupils are sitting alone at the dining room table eating dinner. The grandmother invites the researcher to join them at dinner but he refuses several times. When Mrs. Lewis comes down from upstairs they chat about Thanksgiving. Mrs. Lewis says that the highlight of her vacation was the Ebony Fashion Show at the Ritz-Ambassador for which she had been in charge of selling the top-price tickets which cost $25 apiece. While giving the details about the fashion show and showing pictures of her family and a wedding, she also urges Franklin to stop playing with his food and eat. Instead of eating, Franklin gets up from the table and brings a volume of the *Child's World Encyclopedia* to his mother and asks her to read him a story. She bargains with him, "Oh, not now, Franklin, we'll do it later. You eat first, then I'll read to you." Franklin keeps on begging his mother to read him a story and she insists that he eat something first. Finally, Franklin sits down, but he just plays with his food, cutting it into smaller and smaller pieces. Turning to the researcher his mother says, "You know, if Franklin keeps on doing this, you're going to have to see me feed him just like a baby." Franklin then objects to being called a baby. "Well," says his mother, "If you're not a baby, you're going to have to eat like a young boy, because mothers feed babies." After Franklin continues to play with his food, his mother says with finality, "Well, I guess I'm going to have to feed you. Open up," and she puts a spoonful of spaghetti in his mouth. "Now, chew it." Franklin chews and swallows.

On another occasion, the conversation turns to what Franklin wants for Christmas. "Franklin, what was it you wanted Santa Claus to bring you this year?" Franklin says he wants a Texaco truck, a special police car, a cape, and several other toys and then starts to name some other things. "Oh, no, we can't add any more to the list," says his mother. Franklin replies, "Okay, baby," and his mother looks at the researcher and says, "Did you hear that? He called me 'baby.' This kid just hasn't got any respect for me. You know, it's not unusual. Kids don't have respect for their elders anymore anywhere." At this point she launches into a long discussion of children's lack of respect for others and how difficult it is to handle the problems at school. The grandmother joins the discussion. Mrs. Lewis takes the hard line toward poverty and delinquency against her mother's softer line, saying, "I think if they're doing wrong and they've got a gun, they should be shot right where they are."

At this point, Mrs. Lewis tries to mollify Franklin. "Franklin, you know what? I brought a surprise home for you yesterday and I haven't given it to you. I brought some crayons for you." Franklin perks up and runs upstairs to look for the crayons. As he brings them downstairs with one of his coloring books, he coughs a few times with a deep bronchial cough. His mother looks worried and says, "You know, I've had that boy to see the doctor three times this week, but I might have to take him back again. I had to stay up with him all night a few nights ago, simply because the child had so much difficulty breathing we worried about him. There are children in my classes who come to school with inadequate clothing in the coldest weather, but never seem to catch cold, and here is Franklin, warmly clothed and everything, yet he's sick every so often." Franklin responds to this nonchalantly, "Well, that's the way it goes, baby." This time his mother just frowns and goes on talking about how different people can be.

Several weeks later Franklin is still sick. This time it is his grandmother who is trying to get him to sit down and eat his food. Franklin responds to her nagging, "Okay, baby, whatever you say. I know it's ridiculous, but I'll eat anyway." His grandmother ignores this remark, but his mother says sarcastically, "Okay, cutie pie, you go and show us how you can eat all your food." Franklin comes back with, "Okay, cutie pie, I will, but eating food is ridiculous." Mrs. Lewis explains to the researcher that Franklin vomited last night and she thinks it's because she's been forcing food on him. She wonders what she should do about Franklin's "feeding problem" and says she is just about to give up forcing him to eat.

During a conversation about Franklin later in the year, Mrs. Lewis tells the researcher that she feels she is overprotective of Franklin. She wishes she had the courage to let him go to the "Y," but "What if something happened to him there? A lot of construction is going on there now. What if he fell in a hole?" She doesn't even let him go outside alone or to the corner store for her. If she ever did, she would have to follow him just to make sure that nothing happened to him. Once a neighbor told Mr. Lewis that he would like to take Franklin on a vacation and Fred had replied, "How could that happen when my wife won't even let me take him to Sears?" Mrs. Lewis admits that this is a true picture of how she rears Franklin. "I'm so insecure and uncertain about how to raise this boy . . . I don't even know how to tell my son to walk across the street correctly." This discussion takes place in the presence of Franklin who sits at the table and listens in while making a pen-and-ink picture on legal-size paper of skiers going down a slope. Later he runs to get some of his other drawings to show the researcher. He also spreads out on the floor three murals made out of the ends of wallpaper rolls on which he has pasted pictures cut out of magazines.

Franklin Lewis in School: Teacher's Pet

Franklin is undeniably a favorite of his teacher and the object of her benign interest. She invests almost all of her energy in Pamela and him along with a few of the other very high achievers. He is often made the center of attention in the classroom partly because of the teacher's preference for him and partly because he always brings something to school for Show and Tell. The teacher also depends on him to give the correct answers to her questions even though he frequently lets her down and forces her to turn to Pamela as a last resort to get the particular wording she wants. Since Franklin has already been exposed to a great deal of the content of the kindergarten curriculum at home and at nursery school, he already knows most of it.

Franklin is given more freedom to move around the room and talk when he pleases than any other child in the class, including Pamela. He asserts his right to do this and the teacher rarely stops him. He has the roughhousing traits of most of the other boys, yet the teacher never penalizes him heavily for acting up. In fact she is more likely to blame another child for what he has done when she should have disciplined them both. Occasionally, she comes down hard on him when he tests her patience beyond endurance, but most of the time he demonstrates with his teacher what he has learned so well at home—how to manipulate and be manipulated by the women who are in charge of him. Similar to the manner in which his mother and grandmother treat him at home, his teacher responds to him by giving him a loose rein most of the time and tightening it suddenly and inconsistently when he goes too far.

John and Lee Davidson—Brothers Doing Poorly

John and Lee Davidson, who are six and five years old, live with their great-grandparents, the Russells, in an old house which they purchased recently.[7] Although many of the apartment buildings in the same block are in very poor condition, the Russells are working hard to keep their house painted and in good repair. They have also bought some new furniture and curtains and have plans for adding other pieces. The Russells who are in their mid-sixties were born in the South and have grade-school educations. Mr. Russell is currently a truck driver but has held many other kinds of jobs throughout his life. Even though Mrs. Russell suffers from a debilitating case of diabetes which requires regular treatment at a local clinic, she leads a very active life. She keeps the house very neat and clean and attends a great many services and other programs at her church.

The Russells have taken care of John and Lee since early infancy. They had also reared the children's mother—their granddaughter. The Christmas when John was a month old, his parents asked the Russells to take care of the baby so that they could go out. They never returned to pick him up. When the Russells called to ask their granddaughter when she was coming to get John, her reply was hesitant, so Mrs. Russell told her to bring the baby's crib. It was delivered to the house about 20 minutes later and John has lived with the Russells ever since. The next year the Russells took the second baby, Lee, when he was about two weeks old. Their mother visits the children occasionally, but their father never comes to the house. Mrs. Davidson telephones every other day to see how the boys are and occasionally buys them some clothes, but does not contribute anything else toward their support.

Mrs. Russell made the observation that the boys would be in bad shape if it weren't for her. Indeed, she is very conscientious about looking after them. She does her best to take care of their physical needs, making sure that they eat well, keep clean, and dress properly. She makes a practice of taking the children with her wherever she goes and has never left them at home unattended. Unless they are sitting quietly, however, she acts as if their mere presence is troublesome to her. It is noticeable that she seldom touches the children or talks to them except when she needs to punish them physically or to reprimand them. If the boys are disobedient, she is quick to threaten them with physical punishment and to whip them.

John and Lee spend most of their time alone because Mrs. Russell thinks that the other children in the neighborhood exert a bad influence on them. During the summer she allows them to play in the yard which is fenced in, but she does not permit them to go outside at all when it is too hot because Lee is subject to convulsions when he gets excited and overheated. Wherever they happen to be playing, she checks on them periodically to see that they are not doing anything she considers undesirable.

John is an active and rather aggressive child. Mrs. Russell believes he's the instigator of most of the children's mischievous behavior. For example, the two boys were running around the living room and John jumped on a box and made quite a bit of noise. Mrs. Russell shouted in from outside asking who was making the noise. After a moment of quiet John said that Lee had done it. Mrs. Russell said to the researcher that she thought that John was lying and that she was going to whip him. Although both Lee and John lied very often, in her judgment it was John who lied so quickly. At this point she told John that he was going straight to hell because the Lord said that he would vomit in the face of a liar. This brought tears to John's eyes and both of the boys settled down and kept quiet for a while.

Mrs. Russell seems constantly on the alert for "what they will do next" and whatever it is usually results in punishment, as was the case one morning when she was listening to her pastor's record being played on the radio:

Lee and John got out their book and pretended to read, saying different words. Mrs. Russell asked them what they were doing and Lee said "reading." He then began rolling a car over the book and she told him to stop and to put that car down because he was just toy crazy. She said that he was going to get his hide cut off if he didn't. Lee put the car away and went back to pretending to read. Mrs. Russell then told John to bring his book over to her. He hesitated and said that he wanted to read to himself. Mrs. Russell shouted at him and told him that he couldn't read and to come over so that she could help him. He looked as if he wanted to cry but came over. Mrs. Russell took one sentence from the book and pronounced the words and told John to say them. She then pointed to various letters and he was supposed to tell her what they were. She had to tell him everything and at first he hesitated to speak at all. She went over the words once and then went back over them and asked what she had said. When John couldn't remember on several occasions, she shouted at him and asked him what was wrong. When she got to one letter, she said, "If you don't tell me what this is, Lee is going to see you get a whippin'." She told Lee to get the strap; he got up immediately and brought it over and put it on the couch. She then told John to sit down and she was going to call him back in a few minutes to tell her what that letter was and if he didn't know, he was really going to get it and she told Lee to come over. Lee was very quiet and said everything Mrs. Russell wanted him to while John pretended to read. When

Lee finished, she said, "Lee, you'll do right and John won't." She told John that he was acting up and that Lee was going to learn before him because he would sit down and listen and remember. She said that she was going to let their mother come and teach them because she would beat them good. Lee would do better than John because he at least tried to listen, but John got "the devil in him" and made Lee "act up." She then told them to go upstairs and make their beds.

At another time, when Mrs. Russell, John, and Lee were looking at television, the following episode occurred:

Lee and John got up and went over to the bookshelf and got the three books which they had shown the observer on a previous night. Mrs. Russell asked where the book was that she had begun to show them how to read in. John took out one of the books and recited "Peter, Peter, Pumpkin Eater" from memory. Lee pointed to some pictures of fruit, vegetables and animals and said some of the names. The boys showed the observer the other books and identified quite a few of the pictures in them. Mrs. Russell said she tried to go over the books with them in the morning after they come in from playing, but usually had difficulties because John would have to go to the bathroom or do something else and Lee would have to go to sleep, but she was trying to teach them something about reading before they went to school.

Later in the summer the observer reported the following episode:

John asked the observer to make a snowman and without waiting for his answer, Mrs. Russell told John that there was no snow outside, so how could you make a snowman. When John said he wanted him to draw one on paper, Mrs. Russell said that the observer wasn't going to make any-thing for them because all they did was to tear things up. The boys tried to involve the observer in a few other projects before Mrs. Russell told them to shut up and go outside.

Later in the morning when Mrs. Russell was throwing away two empty plastic bottles, John asked whether he could have them to play with. She handed them to him grudgingly, warning him not to put any sand in them and, if he did, she was going to whip him. John put detergent in one of the bottles and made bubbles by squeezing it. Lee took the other bottle and filled it with sand even though Mrs. Russell had warned the boys not to do this.

John began asking the observer about liking certain foods. Mrs. Russell interrupted him, saying that he asked too many questions, "Children will talk and worry you to death if you let them."

Lee is a more passive and conforming child than John. Neither is he as daring as his brother when it comes to defying Mrs. Russell's orders. However, when she is not around, Lee joins John in doing things which their great-grandmother has told them not to do. On the other hand, when Mrs. Russell is present Lee is quick to tell on John in order to save himself from punishment and he laughs when his brother gets into trouble, as in the following episode:

John took a board which was kept under the steps and put it near the swing set. By stepping on the board, he used it as a ramp to elevate himself to catch the swing bar. Mrs. Russell looked out the door and told him he knew he wasn't supposed to be playing with it. He put the board back where it belonged immediately, but as soon as Mrs. Russell went away from the door, he brought it back. When Mrs. Russell came back to the door and saw both of the boys swinging on the bars, she called to John who ran inside and soon was heard crying. Lee began to laugh and swing on the bars saying, "John's gonna get a good whippin'" and he went to the screen door to watch Mrs. Russell beat John. He was screaming as he received about a dozen licks. When Mrs. Russell finished licking John, she called in Lee who had not expected this and began crying as soon as he got inside. Mrs. Russell sat down in a chair, held him, and beat him on the arms and legs. When she had finished she told him to sit down. Instead he ran into the kitchen. She followed and hit him five more times for running away, after which she turned to the observer and told him that when she gets tired of them, she just beats them up.

John Davidson at School: A Disruptive Child

John Davidson (whom the teacher selected as one of her students who was doing poorly) is outgoing, active, even aggressive, in his classroom behavior. He shows his eagerness to participate by frequently raising his hand and volunteering to recite and take part in classroom activities. He has real trouble conforming to the rigid rules of behavior, often talking without permission and playing when he wants to. He also tries to guess at answers to the teacher's questions when he doesn't know them.

The teacher rarely calls on John to participate in a lesson. Instead she responds to him by punishing him for his aggressive behavior, even though he is good at following directions in most cases. Sometimes during writing and coloring periods, however, he proceeds on his own unless the teacher stops him. John's attempts to be a leader are met with rejection by the other students.

Lee Davidson at School: A Nobody

Lee Davidson, John's brother, is also considered by his teacher to be doing poorly in school. On the periphery of classroom activities, he never volunteers to participate and is seldom called on by the teacher to recite. However, she reprimands him quite frequently. He does not follow the teacher's directions and generally shows little interest in his schoolwork. Although he enjoys playing with the other boys on the fringes of the classroom, he does not act confident or spontaneous and is regarded by them as a follower. He is a rather passive figure in the group.

Jimmy Tayor—A Child Doing Poorly

After several unsuccessful attempts to find Jimmy at home, the researcher decided to walk home with him after school.[8] On the way the researcher asked, "Do you think your mother will be home?" Jimmy nodded and said, "She at home now." But when he rapped on the door, there was no answer. "She not home," he said half audibly. "Where do you go if your mother's not home?" "To a friend." "Where does your friend live?" Jimmy pointed across the street. "Do you know when your mother will be home?" Jimmy shook his head. "Does anybody besides your mother have a key to the house?" "Yes." "How long do you usually stay at your friend's house?" " 'Til my brother and sister come home from school."

At this moment Jimmy's brother approached. "Larry, will your mother be home in the evening?" Dropping his eyes, Larry said softly, "Yes sir." "Is she working?" Larry shook his head and said, "She over at Broome." "Well, does she come home at night?" "Sometimes. Sometimes she stay over there." "Do you think she'll be home Monday night?'' ''Yes sir.'' ''Well, when you see her, would you please tell her that I'm studying the boys and girls in Jimmy's kindergarten and I would like to talk to her and that I'll come back Monday about seven o'clock. Do you think she'll be home then, Larry?'' ''Yes sir.''

A boy who looked like a fourth grader passed by and yelled, ''Jimmy Taylor, where you been? You ain't been in school.'' Jimmy said softly, ''Yes I was.'' The boy spoke to the researcher, ''His mother send him to school but he don't go.'' ''Well, what does Jimmy do when he's not in school?'' ''He walk around the street.''

When the researcher returned to the Taylors' on Monday, Jimmy's sister Bertha let him in. Jimmy was sitting in the middle of a squalid room on a rickety wooden chair. Dirty clothes were piled on the floor and on a couch which was about to collapse. Near the center of the room was an old potbelly stove into which Jimmy kept tossing bits of wood and paper he picked up off the floor. The linoleum on the floor was torn up and filthy. The walls were dirty and much plaster had fallen away. Over the two windows were badly soiled shades, pulled all the way down.

Mrs. Taylor came into the room and spoke to the researcher in a very soft voice, ''Oh, Jimmy said you was comin'.'' She smiled a bit, lowered her head and added, ''But I forgot that you was comin'.'' She went on immediately to talk about her son Larry being in bad trouble: She had spent the day down at the agency trying to straighten out his case. ''Larry is on glue. When he get any money he use it to buy some.'' When she was working, Mrs. Taylor said, Larry did not go to school. He would find some way or other to get some glue. She was afraid that ''they'' were going to put him away. Maybe that would be the best thing for him, because it would keep him away from glue. But she wasn't sure about that. As Mrs. Taylor talked, she kept looking around the room, mumbling, ''I don't know what to do about Larry. I don't know what to do about Larry.''

On another visit the researcher asked Mrs. Taylor how Jimmy was taking to kindergarten. ''Oh, I guess okay, that is, when he go.'' As she answered the question she looked over at Jimmy as if she had given up on him. Whenever she talked to Jimmy or Bertha, she spoke in a very low, unassertive way. She had almost no interaction at all with the two older boys. Asked by the researcher if Jimmy brought home some of the things he did in school, she answered softly, "Sometimes," and began a wandering search among the household debris for some of Jimmy's papers. Eventually, one of the boys rummaged in a chest of drawers and found some papers which were Bertha's and Jimmy's report cards. Bertha's grades were all excellent, mostly ones and twos. The teacher had written the comment, "Bertha is a lovely girl." Mrs. Taylor said, "Oh, she always do good." Jimmy's marks were mostly *P*s and *U*s for poor and unsatisfactory. While this was going on, Jimmy played with the dog and watched the television set intently although the picture was barely visible.

Jimmy, the youngest of the six Taylor children, has two sisters—nine-year-old Bertha and a teenage sister—and three older brothers. Mrs. Taylor is around 40; there is no father in the home. The family is supported by Aid to Dependent Children.

Jimmy Taylor at School: A Needy One

Although Jimmy's teacher selected him as one of the children "doing poorly," his performance in school and his folder of exercises indicate that his work is about average, not poor. Like many of the other children in the class he frequently shows signs of boredom: he is restless, wanders around the room, and stares into space. Jimmy is a quiet child in class, never unruly. Under certain conditions he seems very attentive and eager to recite. Sometimes his teacher praises him for a good performance, but she also frequently fails to respond to his expressions of interest in learning. Although she is more evenhanded and fair in her discipline than the other teachers—she does not neglect the "slow" children or devote a disproportionate share of her attention to the "smart" ones—she has a manner which seems to frighten Jimmy and many others. It is not so much that she is harsh but that she is largely unresponsive to the dependency needs they express when they cry or complain of pain. On a morning when Jimmy walks into the room looking especially forlorn, for example, it is another child, not the teacher, who tries to comfort him by bringing him a puzzle to work on or doing something else to cheer him up.

Although the home life of each of the seven children—Lynn Ames, Emily Burns, Lilly George, Franklin Lewis, John and Lee Davidson, and Jimmy Taylor—was so unique as to almost defy comparison with each other and the 22 other families visited by the observers, there seemed to be some discernible differences in the families of the children selected by the teachers as doing well and doing poorly. It was quite evident that some of the children came from homes which equipped them better than others to achieve success in these schools. It was possible to pick out some conditions and experiences at home which helped or hindered the children in their early school years. The teachers responded positively or negatively to certain kinds of appearances and behavior of the children whose family backgrounds differed in several ways. If a teacher thought that a pupil was doing well, it was likely that his family was better off economically. Franklin Lewis was one of these preferred children whose upper-middle-class teacher happened to move in his family's social circle. Emily Burns's family did not have the economic or social standing of the Lewises, but the adults in her extended family were all employed and upwardly mobile.

Contrasting starkly with the standard of living of the Lewis and Burns households was the dire poverty in which Lilly George and Jimmy Taylor lived. Their teachers regarded them as poor prospects for success in school without ever testing their learning skills. Yet when an observer from the research team devoted a few hours to teaching Lilly and the other George children the alphabet and arithmetic, the children and their mother showed an intense interest in education, and the children made rapid improvements in learning when taught this way. The George children exhibited the kind of ability to concentrate which Maria Montessori had discovered in her *bambini* more than half a century ago. Jimmy Taylor, who lived in dismal surroundings in a family crushed by poverty, acted very attentive in class and was exceedingly eager to participate when his interest was aroused, but his teacher complained bitterly about his truancy and gave him all *P*s and *U*s on his report card. On the other hand, his sister Bertha was described by another teacher as "a lovely girl" and given high marks on her report card. There were some children—almost always girls such as Bertha—who could make up for their poverty by being "lovely." More often than not, however, the children who came to school with the telltale look of poverty were given little help in developing their cognitive abilities.

However, coming to school well dressed and clean did not automatically commend pupils to their teachers. The fact that John and Lee Davidson's great-grandmother kept them and their clothes immaculately clean at all times was not enough to evoke favorable treatment from their teachers. Where there was either harsh discipline or lack of attention by the parents at home, as in the boys' case, the teachers seemed to duplicate the harshness and neglect in the classroom and offered few rewards for learning new ways of relating to adults. Thus, there seemed to be a carryover in the types of relationships of the parents to the child in the home to the types of interaction with the teachers in school. Those children who received high rates of negative response in the classroom also tended to receive high rates of negative response at home. John Davidson, for example, was treated very harshly by both his teacher and his great-grandmother and acted rebellious in both settings. Although John and Lee were both required to be quiet and obedient at home on pain of punishment, Lee's way of dealing with this kind of discipline by his great-grandmother was to be submissive rather than openly rebellious and in the classroom he withdrew to the sidelines.

Those children who were relatively low in the frequency of interaction with their parents—Lynn Ames, Lilly George, and Jimmy Taylor—also tended to be low in frequency of interaction with their teachers. Lynn was usually excluded altogether from her teacher's network of relations, and at home her mother also gave her practically no attention. Lynn's role in her family seemed to be a choice between isolation and playing the part of Cinderella, and her alternatives were startlingly similar in the classroom. For Lilly George, whose harsh but steady mother had shown her own immense sense of deprivation when she snatched the candy bar from her baby, there was at school another overwhelming adult who did not have time for her and allowed her to drift. Bowed down by the crushing burdens of keeping her family of six children going in the face of a most precarious support system, Jimmy Taylor's mother seemed to have given up any hope of curing him of his truancy, an attitude shared by his teacher.

The children defined as doing well by their teachers received a high rate of positive response at home, too. These children were not only surrounded by support and encouragement in their homes, but they had access to adults who were sources of information and guidance about the ways of the larger world. Emily Burns's mother and the entire Burns family unit gave Emily a wealth of attention, care, affection, and firm but kindly discipline. Being provided with rich and varied experiences within her home and outside, Emily had already begun to learn the school way even before entering school. Franklin Lewis was a pampered child in the old-fashioned meaning of the word. Although this was not necessarily a good preparation for being liked by his teachers, Franklin had the special advantage of coming from a family of a higher socioeconomic status than most of the children living in the school district. He had also become adept at relatively sophisticated verbal exchange which made it easier for him to handle the adults in charge of him at school. The reward systems for Emily and Franklin both at home and at school were more positive than negative. In neither place were they exposed to the harsh, punitive, or restricted environments which existed for the other children whether at home or at school.

However, while there was harshness or neglect in many of the homes of the children not doing well, there was also a deep yearning expressed by the mothers for their children to learn and succeed in school. These feelings did not seem to be duplicated in the teachers. Indeed, in a variety of ways, the mothers of the children doing poorly were ferociously protective of their children. However, most of the families could neither prepare their children to be the kinds of pupils the schools would be willing to teach nor were they able to shield them from the feelings of failure learned at school.

Notes

1. Ray C. Rist, *The Urban School: A Factory for Failure* (Cambridge: The MIT Press, 1973), p. 142.

2. Jules Henry, Proposal for Research Submitted to the United States Commissioner of Education, April 1966, pp. 2-5.

3. The case study of Lynn Ames is based on observations and unpublished protocols of Patricia Roberts.

4. The case study of Emily Burns is based on observations and unpublished protocols of Patricia Roberts.

5. Jules Henry, Third Quarterly Progress Report, Project no. 6-2771, Bureau of Research, Office of Education, U.S. Department of Health, Education, and Welfare, 1968, pp. 12-35, and observations by Ray C. Rist were the basis of the case study of Lilly George.

6. *Ibid.*, for the basis of the case study of Franklin Lewis.

7. The case study of John and Lee Davidson is based on observations and unpublished protocols by Patricia Roberts.

8. Jules Henry, Third Quarterly Progress Report, pp. 8-20, and observations by Ray C. Rist were the basis of the case study of Jimmy Taylor.

EPILOGUE

The observations made in the classrooms and homes of black children attending the elementary grades in a midwestern elementary school system were undertaken to understand more fully and at firsthand the educational experiences of black children during their initial years of formal schooling. The schools in this border-state metropolis were segregated—all the members of the student body and the school staff were black. The school district was located in part of the city's large racial and social ghetto.

Using the tools of ethnology, members of a field staff sought to immerse themselves in the lives of the children so that they could witness the processes of learning and not learning as they occurred. The focus of the observations was on the relationships of the children with the significant adults in their lives—their parents and their teachers.

At the time the children were five years old and started kindergarten they became the connecting links between the family and the school. The parents—whether they were biological or social parents, a couple or a single adult—were of course the primary socializers of the children. The schools came into the children's lives during their kindergarten year when each successive group of pupils presented itself at the schoolhouse door for formal instruction. At this juncture the school staff took over important functions in the educational process. The school added to the space of the children's natural habitat, and its personnel were their new part-time caretakers.

Of the seven years spent in the primary grades, there was no year more critical than kindergarten for its influence on the children's subsequent educational careers. Although the pupils' initial exposure to the world of school took place in what might have seemed like innocuous half-day sessions organized around play activities, kindergarten was actually a time of early and fateful reckoning for each child who was about to pass in review before the educator-adults in charge of the schools. It would be misleading to suppose that this first inspection was not a serious business. While equipment in the form of toys and "creative materials" and activities such as singing, games, and dancing might be mistaken for things with which to continue the pastimes of childhood, nothing could be further from the truth. Although from the moment a child entered kindergarten he might have thought he had entered the toy store of his dreams, he had actually come face-to-face with the enormous and unyielding power of the school to make decisions about whether he would qualify as one of the preferred group of pupils who would be granted a chance to learn. Judgments made by the kindergarten teachers about the pupils' educability were made with such finality that few children altered the course they set during the kindergarten year, whether in the direction of success or failure.

The schools regarded themselves as gatekeepers for the upward mobility of the school population. In this role they took the job of examining the applicants for entry into the middle class very seriously. Having attained jobs of responsibility and status in spite of racial barriers, the school staffs felt they were in a position to make decisions about the proper use of scarce resources on behalf of the community. For the benefit of the development of the minority community, even an egalitarian philosophy permitted a choice between helping selected promising individuals and spreading scarce resources among the many. From the teachers' point of view, the allocation of limited supplies would be wasted were they spread evenly among all of the students.

Since a choice was to be made between the promising and the unpromising, the teachers encouraged the evolution of three groups of students who were taught differently and often separately. One group was composed of the fortunate few who entered school socially and cognitively equipped to start learning at the point at which the teachers were prepared to give instruction. These pupils were put in the "high" group seated nearest to the teacher and given a disproportionate amount of teaching time and positive response. A few of these children were the teachers' pets. The rest of the children—the ones who gave off fewer visible signs that they were ready to act in the way the teacher considered essential for learning—were broken up into two groups. In one small group there were usually several boys whom the teachers considered the most troublesome. The teachers interrupted the lessons frequently to put a stop to the "disruptive" activities of these boys and to punish them. They therefore received a lot of attention of a negative sort. The remaining children—who were distributed between the middle and low ability groupings—toed the line more compliantly and did not interfere with the learning of the top group. These were the nobodies who received the least attention of any kind, including both instruction time and discipline.

These early divisions tended to become permanent during the kindergarten year and generally carried over through first and second grade. There was no way of telling whether the teachers' ranking of the children fitted their readiness to learn at this stage since no testing was done until the end of the kindergarten year. Ability grouping is a common practice and research studies show that experienced teachers are good at sizing up their students' academic potential although external and personality factors may influence them unduly. Teachers typically spend more time and effort on their good students than on the rest of the class. In studies of classroom teaching, teachers have been found to give the top fourth of the students in a class the greatest attention and the bottom half, the least attention. According to Benjamin S. Bloom, teachers "unconsciously direct their teaching to some students and ignore others; they give positive reinforcement to some, but not to others. They encourage overt participation from some students, but not from others."[1] However, the preferential treatment of favored students which results in neglect and injury to the less favored is rarely justified by teachers. By and large, teachers do not realize that they are dividing their time and attention so disproportionately among their students. Therefore, although the teachers under observation in our study behaved in ways very similar to most other teachers, at the same time they differed from many other teachers in not hiding their intentions under a credo of equality of treatment. Instead, they openly conducted their classrooms on the assumption that a great many of the children could never learn the curriculum. They did not intend to put much effort into teaching those children who they thought were incapable of learning and in fact did not spend much time trying to involve them in learning.

Having given up on the academic progress of many of the children, the teachers instead spent time on their social and emotional development. The emphasis of this effort was to shape up the class so that the children would learn to become good group members. That so many of the children failed to accomplish this was a matter of continual annoyance to the teachers. As it turned out, learning to recite well, to be responsive to directions, and to act cooperatively with others was not commonly achieved.

In addition, the teachers had different standards for measuring a particular child's progress in learning to participate well in a group. In the high groups which the teachers praised as being cooperative were placed those children whom the teachers seemed to be training to be unsympathetic, bullying types of leaders rather than cooperative group members. The class leaders were rough with the other children, and used threats and force when they did not comply with their orders, but they were not reprimanded for their behavior. If anything, they were copying the punitive ways the teachers treated the students as they kept order in their classrooms, walked through the halls, and lined up for the bell on the playground. Thus, while the teachers verbalized ideals of turning both the unruly and shy children into cooperative members of a group, they were at the same time socializing the favored students in ways quite different from this goal. Although the teachers' pets did not suffer from the growing loss of self-esteem felt by some of the troublemakers and nobodies, their teachers did not seem to worry about the possibility that being encouraged to mistreat other children might have unfortunate consequences for their social and emotional development.

Each classroom of children seemed to be composed of individuals at various developmental stages—some were early bloomers, some were late; many were in between. However, when sorting out the children the teachers did not appear to consider this metaphor of flowers unfolding. Rather, they saw the children as competing for a limited number of parts for which the script was already written. The roles were fairly easy to assign because, as the teachers often remarked, the children fell "so naturally" into them. It was mostly a matter of typecasting. Certain kinds of behavior and appearance commended themselves for the available characters, while others did not. The teachers had learned through experience to recognize those children who could be taught to play the leads. Where there were middle-class and lower-class children in a classroom, it was the middle-class children who almost always qualified as stars. However, some children from low-income homes who acted middle class might also qualify. Where there were no children from middle-class backgrounds in a classroom, the teachers picked out the children who embodied the most middle-classlike behavior. In fact, it would be inaccurate to attribute the differences in teachers' behavior to their perception of the students' social-class position per se, since there was no way of separating their social-class background from the behavioral characteristics that frequently occurred along social-class lines. It was usually the case that the high students were more responsive to the lessons, were socially adept, were verbal and proficient in the use of school language, and showed leadership qualities along with being of a higher status background in almost all instances.

The children who were never in the running as candidates for being taught more than minimally had failed to qualify by being what they were: less pleasing to the adults in the school, less able to demonstrate an appealing combination of personal characteristics, sometimes less mature and more in need of special attention and extra help in mastering the first school lessons, occasionally just less lucky in the competition for the teachers' approval. Alternately ignored and punished by the teacher and directed and demeaned by the class leaders, the nobodies found their classes boring and miserable places to spend their days. Some like Jimmy Taylor managed to play hooky rather frequently. Jimmy would, in the words of a fourth grader in his neighborhood, just "walk around the street" whenever he could manage to slip off and stay out of school without his mother knowing it. Being truant presaged what he would probably do when he was older—drop out of school altogether.

Considering their young age, the pupils who attended these inner-city schools were remarkably good at coping with the conditions they met at school. They took a good deal of enjoyment from being with their friends at school and said that they looked forward to going to school so that they could play with the other children. Despite the bad experiences they suffered at the hands of the teachers and their pet students, the children generally arrived at the school yard in a good mood and rather high spirits. No matter how dismal the school day had been, the children would speak excitedly about an upcoming field trip or a special holiday celebration. When asked to talk about school, the children were exceptionally generous in their opinions of their teachers. Even the students who were often neglected or punished by a teacher would say, "Oh, she all right" and "Yeah, I likes Mis Brown."

As for the teachers' feelings about their work, they said they thought it was important, socially useful, and satisfying and they were proud to be teachers. However, in the observations of the teachers at work in their classrooms, there was daily evidence of how burdensome the task of teaching was for almost all of them. Many complained of being overworked and acted fatigued. Some sat at their desks most of the day, rarely getting up to move around among their pupils. They seemed to be trying to insulate themselves by erecting an impenetrable barrier that would protect them from contact with what they found to be very offensive about many of their students—their ungrammatical speech, their poor clothing, and especially their body odor. This and keeping on top of disciplining the pupils at the same time drained their energy and good humor to very low levels. Teaching became drudgery and worse. As one teacher explained, "I'm really a different person here from at home. At home I have a good disposition."

In an occupation that requires giving so much of oneself to others, these teachers simply did not have resources enough to go around. The psychic costs of the job were so high that the teachers had little energy to spare for the students who could not respond in a satisfying way. The teachers needed replenishment from some-where and they found it in their good students. They needed their comforting response just as much as all the students needed their teacher's attention. They thought they were doing the best job they could, considering the kind of children they had to teach and the poor homes from which the pupils came. They believed that most of the families of the pupils in the school district provided such a bad environment for the children that it was hopeless for the school to try to counteract this. Viewing the students this way, the school staffs felt they were justified in putting most of their time into teaching those children whose potential for learning seemed self-evident in their behavior and performance at the very outset. The children whose initial ways of behaving in school were unresponsive, disruptive, or withdrawn and whose appearance revealed the telltale signs of dire poverty would be taught with the expectation that they could not learn. As the school year wore on and these differences perceived in the children's capacities became realities in their actual performance, the teachers allowed them to drift farther and farther behind rather than redoubling their efforts to keep the slower children going at whatever pace they could.

The teachers' perception of the individual differences among the students had substantial basis in fact. These differences were noticeable almost immediately, even on the first day of school. As the heavy doors of the school buildings swung open in the fall, some of the children entered confidently, chatting with their friends and breaking away from their mothers or older siblings who brought them to the kindergarten rooms. Others held back shyly, sometimes hiding their faces, occasionally crying. Their special styles of approaching life were on display. Each child possessed a distinctive demeanor, appearance, pattern of speech, and manner of relating to other children and adults. It was clear that they had already acquired attitudes, motivations, and skills which would come into play in their school experience. There was also no doubt that each classroom consisted of children with various endowments, strengths, and weaknesses—a range of abilities as yet mostly undeveloped and untested.

Part of the children's individuality stemmed of course from their particular genetic inheritance and part came from living in families with immensely varied patterns of interaction and life styles. What the children from the various families had in common was that they had learned patterns of adaptation to the significant adults in their families which they brought with them to the new situation they faced in the school environment. Sometimes their patterns worked well at school and sometimes they did not. Although the circumstances were different, there seemed to be a considerable carry-over of patterns of child-mother interaction to pupil-teacher interaction. The types of relationships between these pairs of interactors were often remarkably similar. In other words, just as the child elicited certain kinds of responses from his mother, responses which in turn became patterns of interaction, so he elicited similar kinds of responses from the teachers, responses which also became patterned. For example, the child who communicated very little with his mother at home was also quiet and isolated from the teacher. On the other hand, those who seemed to gain the attention at home of his parents or other adults also found the spotlight at school. A child who manipulated his mother tried to do the same at school and seemed to have considerable success. Having learned to cope with their mothers at home in certain ways, whether they turned out to be rewarding or not, the children often used this same adaptation when in school and found that their teachers frequently responded in ways that they had learned to expect from their mothers.

Since the adaptations made to their particular home environments carried over to the school situation, the children did not experience as much discontinuity between the way they were treated at home and the way they were treated at school as might be expected. In these schools at least, the children were not required to completely change over to a strange middle-class set of behaviors that differed sharply from the ones in which they had been reared. In fact, there was a good deal of continuity. This was because their teachers so frequently related to the children in ways they were accustomed to at home. The teachers changed their behavior in accordance with what the individual child elicited, employing subtle variations in kinds of punishments, and rewards which were consonant with a child's early experience and present circumstances.

Faced with the clamorous need for acceptance and recognition by thirty or so children, the teacher managed to interact with almost all of the children in such a way that a stable social structure was established and the class settled down to the routines she wished to impose on the children.

The "stable social structure" in the classroom lowered the amount of student-teacher interaction altogether—a situation considered ideal by the teachers since it signified that they were in control. Consciously or not, the teachers made use of their pupils' ways of relating to the women in charge of them at home, whether the continuation of that relationship was adaptive or maladaptive for the child in a formal learning situation at school. The teachers were confronted with several courses of action which would enable them to teach the children successfully. They could make use of the child-mother interaction pattern as a vehicle for formal instruction or they could work on changing the parts of the pattern which did not seem beneficial to the child's ability to learn. Instead of doing one or the other of these things, the teachers were judgmental about the children's behavior and family relationships. They had a tendency to attribute good qualities to the children with middle-class and middle-classlike patterns of adaptation and bad qualities to the children whose ways of relating demonstrated that they came from lower-class and welfare homes of which they disapproved.

When there were unproductive aspects or dissonance in the relationships between the teachers and their pupils, the teachers seemed to allow the children to take charge of shaping the relationship based on how they had related to significant adults in their lives before entering school. Rather than intervening to create a teacher-pupil interaction that was more conducive to learning, the teachers surrendered their opportunities to be professionally adept at tailoring their services to the characteristics and needs of their clients.

By and large, the teachers' classroom conduct suggested that they had come to terms with a difficult professional assignment in a manner that committed them to an inflexible stance toward the problems encountered in their work, among them the very serious problem of many students' failure to learn to read, write, and do arithmetic in their first three years of grade school. For whatever variety of reasons, these teachers had decided quite openly and with a good conscience to teach only a very few of their pupils and not to teach the rest of them. The failure of so many of the students to acquire even the ordinary beginning skills—ones which do not require unusual intelligence—seemed to stem to a great extent from the teachers' and the schools' inability to respond adequately to the variety of the children's human experiences.[2] Having seen how few of the children were taught, it would be surprising if many of them learned. Having seen how much the pets were taught, it would also be surprising if they had not made good progress in their schoolwork.

Notes

1. Benjamin S. Bloom, *Human Characteristics and School Learning* (New York: McGraw-Hill, 1976), p. 188.

2. George Weber, *Inner-City Children Can Be Taught to Read: Four Successful Schools* (Washington, D.C.: Council for Basic Education, 1971), pp. 25-30, for a summary of the factors that seem to lead to success in reading achievement in the early grades.

BIBLIOGRAPHY

Adams, Bert N. *Kinship in an Urban Setting.* Chicago: Markham, 1968.

Angelou, Maya. *I Know Why the Caged Bird Sings.* New York: Random House, 1969.

Arensberg, Conrad M., and Kimball, Solon T. *Family and Community in Ireland.* Cambridge: Harvard University Press, 1940.

Aries, Philippe. *Centuries of Childhood.* New York: Random House, 1962.

Ausubel, David P., and Ausubel, Pearl. "Ego Development Among Segregated Negro Children." In *Education in Depressed Areas,* edited by Harry A. Passow. New York: Teachers College Press, Columbia University, 1963.

Barker, Roger G., ed. *The Stream of Behavior.* New York: Appleton-Century-Crofts, 1963.

Baughman, E. Earl. *Black Americans: A Psychological Analysis.* New York: Academic Press, 1971.

Bernard, Jessie. *Marriage and Family Among Negroes.* Englewood Cliffs, N.J.: Prentice-Hall, 1966.

Berscheid, Ellen, and Walster, Elaine Hatfield. *Interpersonal Attraction.* Reading, Mass.: Addison-Wesley, 1969.

Billingsley, Andrew. *Black Families in White America.* Englewood Cliffs, N.J.: Prentice-Hall, 1968.

Bloom, Benjamin Samuel. *Human Characteristics and School Learning.* New York: McGraw-Hill, 1976.

———. *Stability and Change in Human Characteristics.* New York: John Wiley, 1964.

Bond, Horace Mann. *The Education of the Negro in the American Social Order.* Reprint. New York: Octagon, 1966.

Bott, Elizabeth. *Family and Social Network.* London: Tavistock Publications, 1957.

Bowles, Samuel. "Getting Nowhere: Programmed Class Stagnation," *Trans-action/Society* 9 (June 1972), pp. 42-49.

Brown, Claude. *Manchild in the Promised Land.* New York: Macmillan, 1965.

Cade, Toni, ed. *The Black Woman: An Anthology.* New York: New American Library, 1970.

Clark, Kenneth B. *Dark Ghetto.* New York: Harper and Row, 1965.

———. *A Possible Reality.* New York: Emerson Hall, 1972.

Clark, Kenneth B.; Deutsch, Martin; Gartner, Alan; Keppel, Francis; Lewis, Hylan; Pettigrew, Thomas; Plotkin, Lawrence; and Riessman, Frank. *The Educationally Deprived.* New York: Metropolitan Applied Research Center, 1972.

Coleman, James S.; Campbell, Ernest Q.; Hobson, Carol J.; McParland, James; Mood, Alexander M.; Weinfeld, Frederick D.; and York, Robert L. *Equality of Educational Opportunity.* Washington, D.C.: Government Printing Office, 1967.

Coles, Robert. *Children of Crisis.* Boston: Little Brown, 1967.

Comer, James P. *Beyond Black and White.* New York: Quadrangle Books, 1972.

Cottle, Thomas J. *Black Children, White Dreams.* Boston: Houghton Mifflin, 1974.

———. *Barred from School: Two Million Children.* Washington, D.C.: New Republic Books, 1976.

Cox, Oliver C. *Caste, Class and Race.* New York: Monthly Review Press, 1948, 1959.

Crain, Robert L. *The Politics of School Desegregation.* Chicago: Aldine, 1968.

Davis, Allison, and Dollard, John. *Children of Bondage.* New York: Harper and Row, 1964 edition.

Davis, Lenwood G. *The Black Family in the United States: A Selected Bibliography.* Westport, Conn.: Greenwood Press, 1977.

Deutsch, Martin, ed. *The Disadvantaged Child: Studies of the Social Environment and the Learning Process.* New York: Basic Books, 1967.

Deutsch, Martin; Katz, Irwin; and Jensen, Arthur R., eds. *Social Class, Race, and Psychological Development.* New York: Holt, Rinehart and Winston, 1968.

Deutscher, Irwin, and Thompson, Elizabeth J., eds. *Among the People: Encounters with the Poor.* New York: Basic Books, 1968.

Drake, St. Clair, and Cayton, Horace R. *Black Metropolis.* New York: Harcourt, Brace and World, 1945, 1962.

DuBois, W. E. B. *The Souls of Black Folk.* Greenwich, Conn.: Crest Reprints, 1961.

Duhl, Leonard J., ed. *The Urban Condition.* New York: Basic Books, 1963.

Ellison, Ralph. *Shadow and Act.* New York: Random House, 1953.

Erikson, Erik H. "A Memorandum on Identity and Negro Youth," *Journal of Social Issues* 20 (1964), pp. 29-42.

Fanon, Frantz. *Black Skin, White Masks.* New York: Grove Press, 1967.

Farber, Bernard, ed. *Kinship and Family Organization.* New York: John Wiley, 1966.

Fasold, Ralph, and Wolfram, Walter. *The Study of Social Dialects in American English.* Englewood Cliffs, N.J.: Prentice-Hall, 1974.

Frazier, E. Franklin. *Black Bourgeoisie.* New York: The Free Press, 1957.

———. *The Negro Family in the United States.* Chicago: University of Chicago Press, 1939, 1948, 1966.

Friedson, Eliot. *Professional Dominance.* Chicago: Aldine, 1970.

Fuchs, Estelle. *Teachers Talk: Views from Inside City Schools.* Garden City, N.Y.: Doubleday, 1969.

Gans, Herbert J. *The Urban Villagers.* New York: The Free Press, 1962.

Geismar, Ludwig L. *555 Families.* New Brunswick, N.J.: Transaction Books, 1973.

Gintis, Herbert. "Toward a Political Economy of Education: A Radical Critique of Ivan Illich's Deschooling Society," *Harvard Educational Review* 42 (1), pp. 70-96.

Glazer, Nathan, and Moynihan, Daniel P. *Beyond the Melting Pot.* Cambridge: The MIT Press, 1963.

Goffman, Erving. *The Presentation of Self in Everyday Life.* New York: Doubleday Anchor Books, 1959.

Goode, William J. *World Revolution and Family Patterns.* New York: The Free Press, 1963.

Gordon, Chad. *Looking Ahead: Race and Family as Determinants of Adolescent Orientation to Achievement.* Washington, D.C.: American Sociological Association, 1972.

Greer, Colin. *The Great School Legend.* New York: Basic Books, 1972.

Grier, William H., and Cobbs, Price M. *Black Rage.* New York: Basic Books, 1968.

Gutman, Herbert G. *The Black Family in Slavery and Freedom, 1750-1925.* New York: Pantheon, 1976.

Hannerz, Ulf. *Soulside: Inquiries into Ghetto Culture and Community.*

New York: Columbia University Press, 1969.

Harris, Seymour, ed. *Educational and Public Policy.* Berkeley, Calif.: McCutchan, 1965.

Haskins, Jim, ed. *Black Manifesto for Education.* New York: Morrow, 1973.

Havighurst, Robert J. *Education in Metropolitan Areas.* Boston: Allyn and Bacon, 1967.

Henry, Jules. *Culture Against Man.* New York: Vintage Books, 1963.

Herndon, James. *The Way It Spozed to Be.* New York: Bantam, 1968.

Herzog, Elizabeth, and Lewis, Hylan. "Children in Poor Families: Myths and Realities." In *Annual Progress in Child Psychiatry and Child Development,* edited by Stella Chess and Alexander Thomas. New York: Brunner Mazel, 1971.

Hill, Robert B. *The Strengths of Black Families.* New York: Emerson Hall, 1972.

Himes, Joseph S. "Some Work-Related Cultural Deprivations of Lower-Class Negro Youths." *Journal of Marriage and the Family* 26 (November 1964), pp. 447-49.

Hollingshead, August B. *Elmtown's Youth.* New York: John Wiley, 1958.

Hope, John, II. *Minority Access to Federal Grants-in-Aid.* New York: Praeger, 1976.

Howard, John R. *The Cutting Edge.* Philadelphia: Lippincott, 1974.

Hunt, J. McVicker. "Black Genes—White Environment." *Trans-action* 6 (June 1969), pp. 12-22.

Hyman, Herbert H. "The Value System of Different Classes." In *Class, Status and Power,* edited by Reinhard Bendix and Seymour Martin Lipset. New York: The Free Press, 1953, pp. 426-42.

Jacobs, Jane. *The Death and Life of Great American Cities.* New York: Random House, 1961.

Jencks, Christopher; Smith, Marshall; Acland, Henry; Bane, Mary Jo; Choen, David; Gintis, Herbert; Heyns, Barbara; and Michelson, Stephan. *Inequality: A Reassessment of the Effect of Family and Schooling in America.* New York: Basic Books, 1972.

Jenkins, Betty, and Phillis, Susan, eds. *Black Separatism: A Bibliography.* Westport, Conn.: Greenwood Press, 1976.

Kahl, Joseph A. *The American Class Structure.* New York: Holt, Rinehart and Winston, 1957.

Katz, Michael B. *Class, Bureaucracy, and Schools.* New York: Praeger, 1971.

Kaufman, Bel. *Up the Down Staircase.* Englewood Cliffs, N.J.: Prentice-Hall, 1964.

Kohl, Herbert. *36 Children*. New York: New American Library, 1967.

Kohn, Melvin L. *Class and Conformity*. Homewood, Ill.: Dorsey, 1969.

Kolko, Gabriel. *Wealth and Power in America*. New York: Praeger, 1962.

Kozol, Jonathan. *Death at an Early Age*. Boston: Houghton Mifflin, 1967.

Kuper, Leo. *Race, Class and Power*. Chicago: Aldine, 1975.

Labov, William. *A Study of Non-Standard English of Negro and Puerto Rican Speakers in New York City*. New York: Columbia University Cooperative Research Project, no. 3288, 1968.

Ladner, Joyce. *Tomorrow's Tomorrow: The Black Woman*. New York: Doubleday, 1971.

Ladner, Joyce, ed. *The Death of White Sociology*. New York: Random House, 1973.

Lemert, Edwin M. *Human Deviance, Social Problems, and Social Control*. Englewood Cliffs, N.J.: Prentice-Hall, 1967.

Leslie, Gerald R. *The Family in Social Context*. New York: Oxford University Press, 1967.

Levine, Donald M., and Bane, Mary Jo, eds. *The "Inequality" Controversy: Schooling and Distributive Justice*. New York: Basic Books, 1975.

Levitan, Sar A.; Johnston, William B.; and Taggart, Robert. *Still a Dream: The Changing Status of Blacks Since 1960*. Cambridge: Harvard University Press, 1975.

Levy, Gerald E. *Ghetto School*. New York: Pegasus, 1970.

Lewis, Hylan. *Blackways of Kent*. Chapel Hill: University of North Carolina Press, 1955.

―――. "Child Rearing Among Low-Income Families." In *Poverty in America*, edited by Louis A. Ferman, Joyce L. Kornbluh, and Alan Haber. Ann Arbor: University of Michigan Press, 1965, pp. 342-53.

―――. "Culture, Class, and Family Life Among Low-Income Urban Negroes." In *Employment, Race and Poverty*, edited by Arthur M. Ross and Herbert Hill. New York: Harcourt, Brace and World, 1967, pp. 149-74.

―――. "Race, the Polity, and the Professions." *Journal of Education for Social Work* (Fall 1969), pp. 19-30.

Lewis, Oscar. *Five Families*. New York: Basic Books, 1959.

Liebow, Elliott. *Tally's Corner*. Boston: Little Brown, 1967.

Litwak, Eugene, and Meyer, Henry J. *School, Family, and Neighborhood, The Theory and Practice of School-Community Relationships*. Chicago: University of Chicago Press, 1974.

Lyman, Stanford M. *The Black American in Sociological Thought*. New York: Putnam's Sons, 1972.

Malcolm X. *The Autobiography of Malcolm X.* New York: Grove Press, 1964.

Marx, Gary T. *Protest and Prejudice: A Study of Belief in the Black Community.* New York: Harper and Row, 1967.

McCall, George J.; McCall, Michal M.; Denzin, Norman K.; Suttles, Gerald D.; and Kurth, Suzanne B. *Social Relationships.* Chicago: Aldine, 1970.

McCord, William; Howard, John; Frieberg, Bernard; and Harwood, Edwin. *Life-Styles in the Black Ghetto.* New York: W.W. Norton, 1969.

Miller, L. P., and Gordon, Edmund W., eds. *Equality of Educational Opportunity.* New York: AMS Press, 1974.

Miller, S.M. "The American Lower Classes: A Typological Approach." In *Blue-Collar World,* edited by Arthur B. Shostak and William Gomberg. Englewood Cliffs, N.J.: Prentice-Hall, 1964, pp. 9-23.

Miller, S.M., and Riessman, Frank. *Social Class and Social Policy.* New York: Basic Books, 1968.

Mosteller, Frederick, and Moynihan, Daniel P., eds. *On Equality of Educational Opportunity.* New York: Random House, 1972.

Myrdal, Jan. *Report from a Chinese Village.* New York: Random House, 1965.

Ogbu, John U. *The Next Generation, An Ethnography of Education in an Urban Neighborhood.* New York: Academic Press, 1974.

Parsons, Talcott, and Clark, Kenneth B., eds. *The Negro American.* Boston: Houghton Mifflin, 1966.

Passow, Harry A., ed. *Education in Depressed Areas.* New York: Teachers College Press, Columbia University, 1963.

Pearl, Arthur. "Schools Versus Kids." In *Among the People: Encounters with the Poor,* edited by Irwin Deutscher and Elizabeth J. Thompson. New York: Basic Books, 1968.

Pettigrew, Thomas F. *A Profile of the Negro American.* Princeton: D. Van Nostrand, 1964.

Piven, Francis Fox, and Cloward, Richard A. *Regulating the Poor.* New York: Pantheon, 1971.

Porter, Judith D. R. *Black Child, White Child, The Development of Racial Attitudes.* Cambridge: Harvard University Press, 1971.

Poussaint, Alvin F. *Why Blacks Kill Blacks.* New York: Emerson Hall, 1972.

Powdermaker, Hortense. *After Freedom: A Cultural Study of the Deep South.* New York: Viking Press, 1939.

Price, Daniel O. *Changing Characteristics of the Negro Population.* Washington, D.C.: U.S. Bureau of the Census, 1969.

Pugh, Roderick W. *Psychology and the Black Experience.* Monterey, Calif.: Brooks/Cole, 1972.

Purcell, Theodore V. "The Hopes of Negro Workers for Their Children." In *Blue-Collar World,* edited by Arthur B. Shostak and William Gomberg. Englewood Cliffs, N.J.: Prentice-Hall, 1964, pp. 144-53.

Rainwater, Lee. *Behind Ghetto Walls: Black Families in a Federal Slum.* Chicago: Aldine, 1970.

Rainwater, Lee, and Yancey, William L. *The Moynihan Report and the Politics of Controversy.* Cambridge: The MIT Press, 1967.

Rist, Ray C. *The Urban School: A Factory for Failure.* Cambridge: The MIT Press, 1973.

Rosenberg, Morris, and Simmons, Roberta G. *Black and White Self-Esteem: The Urban School Child.* Washington, D.C.: American Sociological Association, 1972.

Rosenthal, Robert, and Jacobson, Lenore. *Pygmalion in the Classroom.* New York: Holt, Rinehart and Winston, 1968.

Safa, Helen Icken. *An Analysis of Upward Mobility in Low Income Families.* Syracuse, N.Y.: Youth Development Center, Syracuse University, 1967.

Scanzoni, John H. *The Black Family in Modern Society.* Boston: Allyn and Bacon, 1971.

Schorr, Alvin. *Explorations in Social Policy.* New York: Basic Books, 1963.

Sewell, William H.; Hauser, Robert M.; and Featherman, David L., eds. *Schooling and Achievement in American Society.* New York: Academic Press, 1976.

Sexton, Patricia Cayo. *The American School.* Englewood Cliffs, N.J.: Prentice-Hall, 1967.

———. *Education and Income.* New York: Viking Press, 1961.

Shuy, Roger, and Fasold, Ralph. *Teaching Black Children to Read.* Washington, D.C.: Center for Applied Linguistics, 1969.

Silberman, Charles E. *Crisis in the Classroom.* New York: Random House, 1970.

Silver, Catherine Bodard. *Black Teachers in Urban Schools: The Case of Washington, D.C.* New York: Praeger, 1973.

Singleton, John. *Nichū, A Japanese School.* New York: Holt, Rinehart and Winston, 1967.

Smith, Louis M., and Geoffrey, William. *The Complexities of the Urban Classroom.* New York: Holt, Rinehart and Winston, 1968.

Staples, Robert. *The Black Family.* Belmont, Calif.: Wadsworth, 1971.

Steiner, Gilbert Y. *The State of Welfare.* Washington, D.C.: The Brookings Institution, 1971.

Suttles, Gerald D. *The Social Order of the Slum: Ethnicity and Territory in the Inner City*. Chicago: University of Chicago Press, 1968.

Taeuber, Karl E., and Taeuber, Alma F. *Negroes in Cities*. Chicago: Aldine, 1965.

Talbert, Carol S. "Interaction and Adaptation in Two Negro Kindergartens." *Human Organization* 29 (Summer 1970), pp. 103-14.

Thomas, Piri. *Down These Mean Streets*. New York: Knopf, 1967.

Thurow, Lester C. *Poverty and Discrimination: Studies in Social Economics*. Washington, D.C.: The Brookings Institution, 1969.

Turner, Ralph H. *The Social Context of Ambition*. San Francisco: Chandler, 1964.

United States Commission on Civil Rights. *A Better Chance to Learn: Bilingual-Bicultural Education*. Clearinghouse Publication, no. 51. Washington, D.C.: U.S. Government Printing Office, 1975.

———. *The Federal Civil Rights Enforcement Effort—1974*, vol. 3. *To Ensure Equal Educational Opportunity*. Washington, D.C.: U.S. Government Printing Office, 1975.

———. *Racial Isolation in the Public Schools*, vol. 1. Washington, D.C.: U.S. Government Printing Office, 1967.

Valentine, Charles. *Culture and Poverty: Critique and Counter-Proposals*. Chicago: University of Chicago Press, 1968.

Weinberg, Meyer. *Minority Students. A Research Appraisal*. Washington, D.C.: U.S. Government Printing Office, 1977.

Willie, Charles V., ed. *The Family Life of Black People*. Columbus, Ohio: Charles E. Merrill, 1970.

Winch, Robert. *Identification and Its Familial Determinants*. Indianapolis: Bobbs-Merrill, 1962.

Wright, Richard. *Black Boy*. New York: Harper and Row, 1945.

Yetto, Samuel F. *The Choice: The Issue of Black Survival in America*. New York: Putnam, 1971.

Young, Michael, and Willmott, Peter. *Family and Kinship in East London*. London: Routledge and Kegan Paul, 1957.

INDEX

ABOUT THE AUTHOR

Helen Gouldner, Dean of Arts and Sciences and Professor of Sociology at the University of Delaware, coauthored *Modern Sociology* and has published in *Trans-Action* and the *Administrative Science Quarterly*.

DATE			
FE 6 '81			
AP 15 '82			
OC 26 '93			